Southeast Alaska's
Natural World

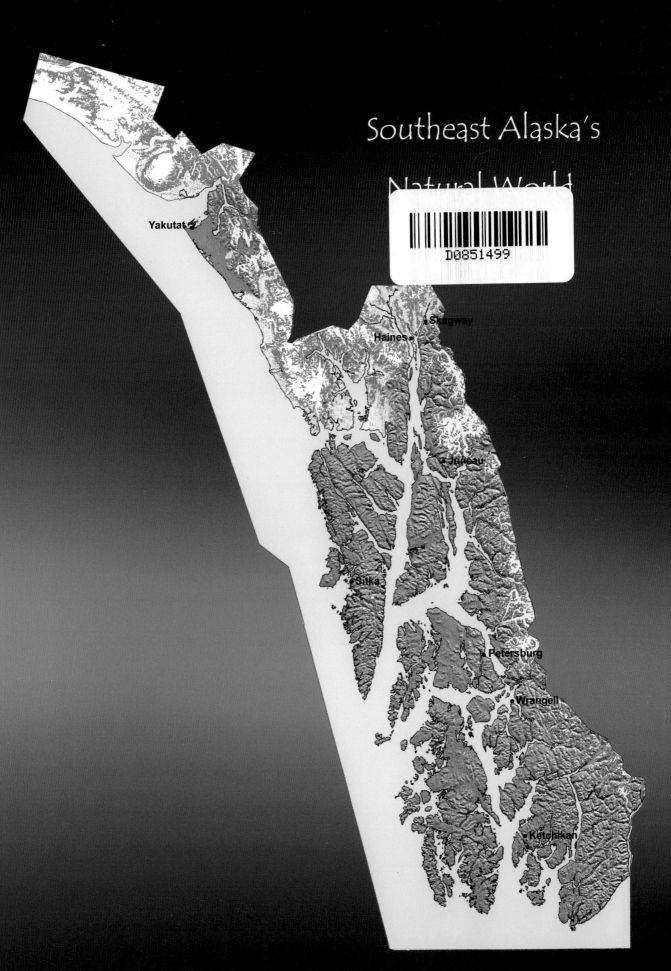

Yakutat

Skagway
Haines

Juneau

Sitka

Petersburg

Wrangell

Ketchikan

OTHER BOOKS
BY THESE AUTHORS:

By Robert H. Armstrong and Marge Hermans

Alaska's Natural Wonders

By Robert H. Armstrong

Guide to the Birds of Alaska

Alaska's Birds: A Guide to Selected Species

Alaska's Fish: A Guide to Selected Species

By Rita M. O'Clair, Robert H. Armstrong, and Richard Carstensen

The Nature of Southeast Alaska:

A Guide to Plants, Animals, and Habitats

Roger W. Pearson and Marjorie Hermans, Editors

Alaska in Maps: A Thematic Atlas

Black Oystercatcher

Southeast Alaska's Natural World

Robert H. Armstrong
and
Marge Hermans

This book is dedicated to all those who treasure
the natural world of Southeast Alaska,
and to the researchers who have contributed to our knowledge about it.

This publication ©Robert H. Armstrong & Marge Hermans 2004
Photographs ©Robert H. Armstrong

Pre-press and Distribution: Todd Communications, Anchorage, Alaska
Printing: Samhwa Printing Co., Seoul, Korea

Copies of this book may be purchased through Todd Communications,
203 W. 15th Ave., Suite 102, Anchorage, AK 99501 USA. Phone: (907) 274-8633

Printed in Korea
First printing, October 2004
10 9 8 7 6 5 4 3 2 1

ISBN 1-57833-270-2
Library of Congress Control Number: 2004096753

Contents

Introduction

He ran from the house, leaped on his horse, and rode off in all directions. This infamous "quote" describes how we often feel when we encounter the natural world here in Southeast Alaska. There is so much to see, so much to do, so much to learn, and so much to think about—the possibilities seem endless. And indeed they may be.

For most people, Southeast Alaska evokes images of humpback whales, lumbering brown bears, bald eagles, and perhaps sea otters. But beneath this large-scale panorama countless other living things thrive and interact. Creatures and processes simmer and stir amid the waterways, mountains, muskegs, and rainforest. Shorebirds probe the mud and shallows. Forest birds flit amid trees and understory shrubs. Wildflowers bloom, mosses soak up raindrops, marmots hibernate for winter then emerge in spring. Hawks skim the beach meadows in search of prey. Lichens parcel out the decades on alpine rocks and newly exposed glacial forelands.

This book explores just a few of these wild inhabitants and processes—subjects that have especially sparked our interest over the years we've lived in Southeast. Most of the "stories" collected here began as articles we wrote for the *Alaskan Southeaster* magazine, where we sought to share the excitement of the Southeast natural environment with readers inside Southeast Alaska and beyond. From the outset we felt we were writing for our neighbors—residents of Southeast who were interested in learning more about their surroundings; former residents who still reminisced or dreamed about their time in Southeast; and visitors who came to learn about a place that offered fresh horizons and sometimes fulfillment of a lifelong dream.

American emerald dragonfly emerging from its larval exoskeleton

In our explorations we drew from a variety of experiences—Bob's as an ecologist, scientist, and photographer trained to observe his surroundings; Marge's as a writer and lover of the outdoors fortunate to divide her time among three different locations in Southeast Alaska. Usually our observations raised more questions than they answered, and we spent many hours researching information to learn more about what we'd observed.

Female goshawk on nest

Sometimes we found people with extensive knowledge of the areas we were exploring—people who spent their lives studying dragonflies, or what makes nesting eagles successful, or what insects threaten Southeast forests. Sometimes we interviewed them, and their generosity in sharing their knowledge and enthusiasm added immensely to the information we had gathered.

The final satisfaction (and challenge!) came in trying to put what we had learned about each subject into narratives and photographs that would convey what we'd learned to all those neighbors we feel we are writing for.

We hope readers will enjoy our stories, and that our words and images will foster new understandings. Perhaps they'll also prompt some exciting explorations.

All of us who spend time in Southeast are tremendously fortunate to enjoy an area where many natural systems still function as a whole, and where the natural world is a vital and integral part of many people's lives. For the sake of future generations and our own, we hope that will always be so!

Robert H. Armstrong
Marge Hermans
Juneau, Alaska

Amphibians

Western Toad

Amphibians in Southeast Alaska

Almost everywhere in Southeast you come across ponds that look like good places to see frogs, toads, and salamanders. The bogs scattered throughout our landscape are dotted with small ponds. Meandering rivers on the mainland create ponds. Beavers create ponds. Retreating glaciers leave pothole ponds. And post-glacial uplift forms ponds from what once were tidal sloughs. No wonder Southeast is home to eight species of amphibians.

Six of these species are native to Southeast: the **western toad**, the **Columbia spotted frog**, the **wood frog**, the **rough-skinned newt**, the **northwestern salamander** and the **long-toed salamander**. Western toads and rough-skinned newts are widespread in the region and are found on many islands. Spotted frogs, wood frogs, and long-toed salamanders are found mostly along mainland rivers such as the Taku and Stikine. Northwestern salamanders have been found at only three localities: on Mary Island southeast of Ketchikan, near Pelican, and at Graves Harbor on the outer coast.

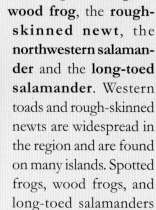

Juvenile wood frog

Two other species—Pacific tree frogs and red-legged frogs—were introduced. Tree frogs have established a breeding population near Ward Lake in Ketchikan, and one was recently found in a pond in Juneau. Red-legged frogs were introduced into a pond near Hoonah on Chichagof Island and are now successfully reproducing and dispersing into adjacent wetlands.

Columbia spotted frog

We wrote articles on rough-skinned newts and western toads for two different reasons.

One day a friend of ours in Juneau called and said, "Some of my son's friends are finding lots of newts near Tee Harbor. Do you want to see them?" We did, and the kids' enthusiasm rubbed off on us. Subsequent research led us to the outstanding work of researchers Edmund D. Brody, Jr. and Edmund D. Brody III, who generously shared their findings and responded to our many questions.

We wrote about toads for a much sadder reason: They seemed to be disappearing from around our home town. Several friends in Ketchikan, Wrangell, and Gustavus said they'd noticed severe declines, too. Our search to discover why led us to research that implicated global warming and a fungus as possible causes of toad declines in other parts of the United States. So we wrote to Gary Laursen, a fungus expert at the University of Alaska in Fairbanks, who referred us to a thick book titled *Fungi and Environmental Change*.

Long-toed salamander

Shortly afterward, Bob collaborated with Richard Carstensen and Mary Willson in a two-year study of amphibians in Southeast. The final report from that study is available over the internet at discoverysoutheast.org. Other excellent sources of information include Robert Parker Hodge's *Amphibians & Reptiles in Alaska, the Yukon & Northwest Territories* (now out of print but available in most Alaska public libraries); and *The Amphibians and Reptiles of Alaska: A Field Handbook* by S. O. MacDonald, which provides the most comprehensive and current information on the distribution of amphibians in Alaska. This handbook can be downloaded from the U.S. Fish and Wildlife Service, Juneau Field Office, at http://alaskaherps.info

Newts
in the Rainforest

Southeast Alaska, home of bald eagles, brown bears, humpback whales, and . . . *what?* **rough-skinned newts?**

Not many tourism brochures wax poetic over the fact that you might find small, four-legged, long-tailed amphibians under rocks and logs in parts of Southeast. But for some folks finding small critters like these generates as much excitement as seeing whales bubble-net feeding or brown bears wrestling salmon from a stream.

We first heard that newts were being found in the Juneau area from our friend Dick Wood. He told us some buddies of his son Evan had been finding newts in the woods and in a marsh close to Tee Harbor. One day in July we met two of the boys, Eric and Brendan Daugherty, and their mom Susan. They took us into the woods to see for ourselves.

That day the boys found the first newt under a rock in the woods not far from the highway. The small, quick-moving critter was about four inches long. The skin on its sides and back was dark brown, with the rough, pebbly look that gives the species its name, *Taricha granulosa.* Its underside was a brilliant orange-yellow. With its four strong legs and long tail, it looked for all the world like a miniature dragon that had escaped from some children's fairy tale.

As Dick held up the half-rotted chunk of wood we'd placed it on, the newt clambered up and over its ridges and crevices, rearing up and peering intently about as if to get the lay of the terrain so as to end this ridiculous exercise of being ogled and pointed at by a gaggle of babbling giants.

While we were looking at the newt we met up with two other boys from the neighborhood, Henry and Daniel Melville. We put Newt #1 back under its rock and split

Rough-skinned newts have orange-yellow bellies—a warning to predators that this animal is toxic.

Henry and Daniel Melville (left to right) have found many newts in a marsh near their home in Juneau.

into two groups to trudge up to the marsh where the boys said they'd often found quite a number of newts.

The boys had apparently learned something about newts in school, and it was obvious they'd also done a lot of study and research on their own. Some of them had kept newts in aquariums and watched them until their parents insisted they return them to the wild.

Daniel said he had watched a female laying eggs in the water—"laying eggs everywhere!" and says he saw some hatch and watched the babies try to move, "wiggling their tails about four or five times a second."

Henry told us that in winter newts go into the mud at the bottom of the marsh, their breathing and heartbeat slow down, and they don't eat. "How do you know that?" we asked him. He said his brother Daniel told him. Susan wondered why the newts were found in this particular place and said several people had told her they remembered finding newts on Shelter Island near Juneau.

We found it exciting to see the beautiful marsh—filled with yellow pond lilies and bordered with buckbean, Alaska cotton, and even a large patch of poison water hemlock.

It looked like ideal habitat for newts, which return to quiet water with aquatic vegetation for breeding. This is the area where the boys have found sometimes a dozen newts under a single board.

We enjoyed seeing the boys' excitement over finding these fascinating critters and learning about them, whether at school, from the internet, or from watching the animals themselves. But things got even more interesting once we started tracking down more information about these shy amphibians.

"The most poisonous salamander on the planet"

We learned that some rough-skinned newts are among the most poisonous animals in the world. They secrete *tetrodotoxin* *(TTX)*, one of the most potent neurotoxins known to science, from glands in their skin. The toxin is a defense against animals that typically eat small amphibians—predatory birds such as hawks, owls, jays, or herons; fish; mink, shrews, snakes, or even bears.

Besides making newts distasteful, TTX causes animals that ingest it to gasp, regurgitate, and suffer convulsions and paralysis. Most predators that ingested a toxic newt would in fact die, perhaps even before the newt did. The rough-skinned newts' bright

Where Are the Newts?

Rough-skinned newts range from the San Francisco Bay area in California to southern Alaska. They live generally west of the crest of the Cascade Range, from sea level to about 9,000 feet elevation.

Newts have been reported in coastal forests throughout Southeast Alaska, and have been found on Admiralty, Prince of Wales, Annette, and Shelter Islands; at Ward Lake near Ketchikan; at Wrangell Reservoir; and near Tee Harbor north of Juneau.

A Newt's Life

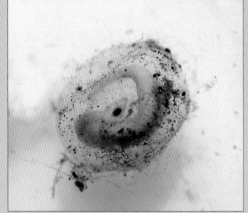

(Upper left) Newt eggs are very tiny—about one-tenth of an inch in diameter. Note the tiny developing larva inside the egg.

(Upper right) This newt larva is about one inch long and in its first summer.

(Lower photo) This newt larva is nearly two and a half inches long and is probably about two years old. Soon it will transform into an adult.

Adult rough-skinned newts live most of the year on land, but they return to the vegetated fringes of lakes, ponds, or slow-moving streams to breed. The female attaches single eggs onto the undersides of vegetation, where they are difficult to find. Sometimes they are "glued" between the leaves of vegetation so they remain hidden from predators.

The eggs hatch in five to 10 weeks, producing larvae that have feathery gills and live in the water. In their first or second summer, the larvae change form and move out of the water onto land.

Adult newts generally return to the water's edge to breed, perhaps in their fourth or fifth year. They sometimes travel in groups and along traditional "highways."

Long-term survival of newts in Southeast Alaska will probably depend on maintaining the combination of habitats they need to complete their aquatic/terrestrial life cycle.

yellow-orange undersides are nature's warning of toxicity (much like the yellow and black bands of wasps and bees, or the bright colors of some frogs and insects). Most animals, except the common garter snake, seem to pay attention to the warning and scratch newts off their lists of potential meals.

As we read more studies we learned that tests on laboratory mice have shown TTX is weight-for-weight 10 to 100 times as lethal as black widow spider venom and more than 10,000 times as lethal as cyanide. It has the same toxicity as *saxitoxin*, the neurotoxin that causes paralytic shellfish poisoning. Studies have shown that one adult newt can produce enough toxin to kill about seven humans.

TTX is the toxin found in pufferfish, sometimes specially prepared as raw "sashimi fugu" or in a soup called "chiri," as a kind of dining adventure for the brave or foolhardy in Japan. It is found in a variety of other marine life, including certain sea stars, octopus, parrotfish, and horseshoe crabs, and in the South Atlantic sea squirt.

A single milligram or less of TTX—the amount that could be placed on a pinhead—is sufficient to kill an adult human, and indeed it has done so when people have ingested it. Several bizarre incidents of TTX toxicity were reported in the journal *California Wild*:

• In July 1979, a 29-year-old college student in Oregon suddenly collapsed at a party; not long afterwards he was dead. An autopsy revealed the remnants of a rough-skinned newt in his stomach. Apparently, he had swallowed the amphibian on a dare.

• In 1996, three chefs in southern California collapsed within minutes of eating very small amounts of pufferfish brought back from Japan by a co-worker. They were rushed by ambulance to a local emergency room, where all three eventually recovered.

• In May 1998, two women nearly died after eating pufferfish in a Los Angeles restaurant. For awhile they were totally paralyzed and required artificial ventilation in an intensive care unit for two days.

Both the Los Angeles women recovered, but the Downstate Medical Center in Brooklyn estimates that between 100 and 200 people a year become seriously intoxicated from TTX, and about half of them die, even with treatment.

Recent studies suggest that in some animals TTX may be generated by bacteria. Whether or not the toxin in newts is produced by bacteria is not yet known, but researchers are working to find out.

A predator and prey "arms race"?

In other research, scientists have learned that one predator—*Thamnophis sirtalis,* the common garter snake—has developed a resistance to TTX. While other predators that eat rough-skinned newts "virtually always die," as one study stated, this one species of garter snake continues to feed on rough-skinned newts wherever their ranges overlap.

When a garter snake swallows a newt, it may be immobilized for up to seven hours while the powerful TTX attacks its nervous system. But eventually the snake recovers. There are hazards involved for the snake. It may be caught by one of its own predators while it is immobilized, or it may overheat and die in the sun because it is unable to thermoregulate. But after its brief period of immobility it appears to return to normal— and "normal" for these garter snakes seems to include further dining on rough-skinned newts despite suffering toxic effects.

As part of investigating this odd behavior, scientists have learned that not all newts are equally toxic. Biologists Edmund D. "Butch" Brody, Jr. at Utah State University, and Edmund D. Brody III at Indiana University have been studying the toxicity of rough-skinned newts and how it relates to TTX-resistance in garter snakes in areas where their ranges overlap. Thus far they have found that some populations of newts are many times more toxic than others. They've also found that where newt popula-

A Cautionary Note

According to Robert Stebbins and Nathan Cohen, the authors of *A Natural History of Amphibians*, the ordinary handling of newts has not caused any poisoning in humans. To take effect, the toxin must enter the digestive track or get into the blood stream.

Biologist Edmund D. Brodie, Jr., who has done extensive research on newts, once wrote that while handling them he has accidentally touched his fingers to his tongue and mouth and experienced "a severe burning sensation." He told us he recommends that "people should wash their hands after handling newts, and if they have serious cuts on the hands, not handle newts. I have handled thousands of newts without ill effect. Because TTX is water soluble it washes off easily."

tions are most toxic, the garter snakes that feed on them have developed the greatest resistance to TTX.

Thus far, the Brodies have found that newt toxicity varies by geographic area, and garter snake resistance to toxicity seems to correlate with it. Newts from the San Francisco Bay area are the most toxic, and garter snakes there are almost 100 times more resistant to TTX than snakes in any other populations sampled. Newts tested in Oregon are also highly toxic, and common garter snakes (which feed on them there) are 10 to 30 times as resistant to TTX as snakes from populations outside the range of newts. Newts from Vancouver Island and the Olympic Peninsula of Washington state have very low levels of TTX, and some have none at all. The garter snakes that feed on them also show hardly any TTX resistance.

Resistance to TTX appears to be genetically determined and thus inherited over generations. The Brodies think that garter snake populations may be evolving to overcome newt defenses, and newt toxicity may be escalating as the snakes evolve resistance.

Newts in Southeast

Since the Brodies' work seems to show newt toxicity decreasing as you move north through their range in the Lower 48 and British Columbia, we wondered if newts from Southeast Alaska, the northermost part of their range, would be toxic at all. We sent several live newts from the Tee Harbor area to "Butch" Brodie, and to everyone's surprise, the newts did turn out to be toxic. This disrupts the idea of any orderly progression in level of toxicity from north to south. It also raises a number of questions.

Do all newt populations in Southeast exhibit the same levels of toxicity? What animals, if any, eat newts here in Southeast,

where garter snakes do not occur? And are any predators here resistant to the TTX in our newts?

We don't have answers to these questions, but we may have them someday. Scientists have been studying TTX since the mid-1960s, because of its possible implications for human medicine. They know that TTX binds to sodium ion channels along the peripheral nerves of animals yet does not appear to reach the brain to affect consciousness and mental functions. Among other possibilities, their findings are leading to the development of drugs to block pain from chronic inflammation and nerve injuries without side effects.

The courtship sequence of newts has also been studied as a key to understanding hormonal bases of reproductive behavior.

Perhaps some youngster fascinated by small amphibians near his or her rainforest home will grow up to study and find the answers to tantalizing puzzles like these. That would be a fitting acknowledgment of the importance of one of Southeast Alaska's lesser known, less spectacular animals.●

Rough-skinned newts are named for the small bumps on their skin. Their skin is thick and roughened by numerous closely set tubercles, or small warts (except in males in breeding condition, whose skin becomes smooth and puffy.) Newts have four toes on their forefeet, and five on their hind feet.

Toads in Southeast Alaska

Adult western toads spend most of their time on land.

When toads return to fresh water for mating, the male toad (in the rear) grips the female tightly around her upper belly. He has enlarged thumbs with roughened areas on top for hanging on.

If you're walking in the woods and meadows in Southeast and a chunky, frog-like creature walks or hops away from your footsteps, you're probably seeing a western toad. These are the only toads found in Alaska; and of the seven kinds of amphibians found in Southeast Alaska, they are the ones that have been most abundant and widespread throughout our region.

Western toads are squat and chunky (not so slender and streamlined as Southeast's spotted and wood frogs), and they have warts on their skin. Individual toads may range in color from brown to green or gray. They generally have a light colored vertebral stripe down the back and an underside that is white mottled with black spots. Adults may grow to as much as three and a half inches long, so they are almost the size of a typical computer "mouse."

Toads are found on the Southeast Alaska mainland, on Admiralty, Baranof, and Chichagof Islands, and probably on most other islands in the region. Adult toads live on land, but in spring they migrate to freshwater ponds to mate.

In shallow water, females lay long strings of bead-like eggs that hatch into tadpoles—small black larvae with rounded bodies and long tails. Tadpoles live in the

water for about two or three months, feeding on algae and organic debris, and breathing through gills. By late summer they are ready to leave the water. They resorb their tails and "metamorphose" into tiny toadlets with developed lungs, skin glands, and four legs with webbed toes.

Once toadlets take to the land, they disperse to woodlands, meadows, and muskegs, where they feed on insects and other small animals. They may even be found at high elevations. Ed Grossman, a biologist with the U.S. Fish and Wildlife Service in Juneau, reported that he saw juvenile toads above 3,000 feet along the Taku River when he was mountain goat hunting.

Despite any old wives' tales you might have heard, touching toads doesn't give you warts. But there is a grain of scientific truth that might have prompted such stories. Toads and other amphibians have remarkable glands scattered throughout their skin or grouped in the warts and parotoid glands behind their ears. These glands give off secretions that not only keep the toads' skin moist but also are distasteful to predators and may even cause toxic symptoms if they're swallowed.

The eggs of western toads are also distasteful and possibly toxic, at least in the early stages of egg development, and this discourages predators from eating them. Newly hatched tadpoles may retain some of these chemical defenses, but once they become more mobile the tadpoles tend to lose their noxious properties.

At this time, however, another rather remarkable defense mechanism kicks in. Tadpoles that are injured (as in attacks by predators) release an odorous alarm substance, which causes other tadpoles nearby to flee and presumably escape being eaten. Also, certain tadpoles in each batch release a growth-inhibiting substance that acts on smaller tadpoles so that tadpoles in a single group metamorphose into toadlets in waves

Toad larvae, or tadpoles, live in fresh water for two or three months. They usually school together in shallow, warm water.

rather than all at once. This makes it less likely that an entire generation of tadpoles and toadlets would be destroyed by mass predation or unfavorable events affecting their environment.

A number of creatures in Southeast Alaska no doubt eat toads, especially tadpoles during their non-toxic stages. Dragonfly and water beetle larvae, mallards, greater yellowlegs, great blue herons, mink and river otter probably take advantage of their occasional abundance. Usually predators eviscerate adult toads and leave the toxic skin behind. In fact, people in Southeast have occasionally reported seeing piles of eviscerated toad skins, probably leftovers from meals of ravens, crows, or gulls.

Robert Parker Hodge, author of *Amphibians and Reptiles in Alaska, the Yukon and*

A young, recently metamorphosed toadlet heads out on its own and will live a solitary life until it returns to fresh water to mate.

Before dispersing from their natal ponds, toadlets sometimes congregate in mounds that may number in the hundreds. They perhaps do this to avoid dehydrating.

Western toads are easily recognized by the numerous bumps, or warts, on their skin and parotoid glands behind their ears.

Northwest Territories, reported gulls preying on breeding toads near Ketchikan. He wrote, "The bodies of eviscerated toads litter the pond margins during the breeding season."

Mysterious Disappearances

Recently scientists and private citizens in many parts of the world have reported that the numbers of amphibians such as toads and frogs have been suddenly and drastically decreasing. No long-term studies have been done in Southeast, but many people say they have noticed unusual declines.

We both remember seeing what Hodge describes in his 1976 book about amphibians: "Waves of metamorphosing toads are readily observed during July-August in small ponds in the Juneau area. The pond margins are often so littered with minute toadlets that it is impossible to take a step without crushing several individuals." But that was years ago, and neither of us has seen such a sight recently.

In a study of western toads along the Juneau road system, Bob and two other researchers looked at 270 ponds. They found breeding toads in only six of them, and toad numbers appeared to be quite small.

"Toads used to be widespread in most habitats around Gustavus," Greg Streveler, a long-time Gustavus resident, told us. "They were especially common in the woods, ponds, and side sloughs. Nowadays they are very scarce, and I only see one now and then." We have received similar reports of declines from longtime residents of Ketchikan and Wrangell.

Apparently western toads are still abundant in some parts of Southeast. Ed Grossman of the U.S. Fish and Wildlife Service told us while he and John Lindell were doing surveys for Columbia spotted frogs during 1993-1998, they found numerous western toads along the Salmon River near Hyder, along Grant Creek in Misty Fiords, and along the Taku River.

Amphibian populations naturally show large fluctuations, and declines are not always consistent over large areas. Yet, even allowing for natural fluctuations, populations in many different parts of the world have severely declined. Some declines have been clearly linked to habitat destruction, but others are not associated with obvious environmental factors.

Among the known and suspected causes of declines are:

• introduction of predators or competitors into certain areas,

• increased ultraviolet radiation due to thinning of the world's ozone layer,

• environmental pollution, including acid rain and snow,

• adverse weather patterns,

• infectious disease,

• or a combination of many different factors.

It is especially puzzling that some of the declines are in relatively "pristine" areas such as untouched tropical rain forests in Australia and Central America.

Bruce Wing from the National Marine Fisheries Service Auke Bay Biological Laboratory in Juneau told us he had one report of a large dieoff of western toads near Juneau, but before anyone could get out to collect any to study, they had been cleaned up by scavengers.

Wing said he wonders if a decline of toads in Southeast might be due to the warming trends and lack of snowfall at lower elevations in recent years. In winter toads hibernate underground. Without adequate snow cover during cold snaps, they may be subjected to more freezing than they can withstand.

We propose another theory for Southeast. Perhaps our toads are being attacked by a fungus. Chytrids are fungi found in aquatic habitats and moist soil, where they degrade cellulose, chitin, and keratin, important substances found in living organisms.

According to Dr. Gary Laursen, the fungal expert at the University of Alaska Fairbanks, these "water molds" are very common throughout Southeast's coastal rainforest. Parasitic chytrids infect mainly plants, algae, protozoa, and invertebrates. However, they have recently been implicated in mass deaths of amphibians in Australia and Panama; in mass die-offs of western toads in Colorado; and in the disappearance and presumed extinction of the recently discovered golden toad (*Bufo periglenes*) of Costa Rica. These are the first known instances of chytrids attacking vertebrates.

But if chytrids are widespread in Southeast forests, and if our toads have presumably been living with them for generations, why might they suddenly be killing off the toads? Perhaps the chytrids have become more prevalent or more virulent, like the viruses that have evolved in response to antibiotics. Or perhaps the fungi are attacking toads when their natural defenses are down.

J.C. Frankland and G.M. Gad write in the book *Fungi and Environmental Change*, "Environmental change may influence the behavior of a fungus directly. Abnormally high winter temperatures cause the fungus to be active for a longer period than normal,

Golden toads (Bufo periglenes) from Costa Rica may now be extinct because of a fungus similar to those commonly found in Southeast Alaska forests. The toad on top is the male.

Color and wart patterns can vary considerably among individual toads.

while the host's defense mechanisms are not yet active."

If warmer weather in Southeast is allowing the chytrids found throughout the forests to be more active than they used to be in winter—when toads are hibernating and their defenses are low—it's possible our toads are vulnerable to the fungus now, though they have not been in the past. As Frankland and Gad write, "The balanced relationship between host and fungus is disrupted."

Only further time and study will show why toads in Southeast seem to be declining—and whether or not the decline will continue. It is sad to speculate about the possible ripple effect of toads vanishing or becoming extremely rare in Southeast. Mosquitoes and flies may be happier, but river otters, ravens, great blue herons, dragonfly larvae, and predacious diving beetles may have to look a little harder for an easy meal. And one more fascinating piece of nature will be missing for all the residents and visitors who go out walking in the woods.

Reluctant Pioneers

Western toads are found in a wide variety of settings in Southeast Alaska. After studying toads in Glacier Bay, researcher Michael S. Taylor wrote, "The boreal [western] toad may make full-time use of more habitats than any other vertebrate species in Glacier Bay. . . . Almost any area with insects, a pond suitable for reproduction, and rocky or vegetative cover providing adequate freeze protection appears to suffice."

Taylor suggests that toads are "a very successful pioneer animal"—though probably not intentionally. He found that, although Glacier Bay has a wet, maritime climate like the rest of Southeast, each summer there are usually a few periods of a week or more when the weather is sunny and dry. At those times, some toads move into swift glacial streams to hydrate, or take on the water they need to survive.

But once in these streams, where water temperatures average around 35° to 39°F, the toads rapidly lose body heat. Becoming weak and poorly coordinated, they can no longer swim back to shore. They are swept downstream and out into the salt water of the bay.

The salt water is usually warmer (perhaps 42° to 50°F), and as the toads warm up, their coordination returns and they begin to swim. Ironically, sea water would eventually dehydrate and kill a toad. But Taylor showed that a well hydrated toad can survive several hours in seawater—enough time to reach new land.

By the time they reach shore, the reluctant adventurers may have been carried a mile or more, and perhaps they end up on land so recently deglaciated that they are the first of their species to set foot on it.

The process Taylor describes, or one similar to it, may explain how toads have managed to become established on virtually all the islands in Southeast Alaska.●

Birds

Greater Yellowlegs

Birds in Southeast Alaska

Varied thrush

Southeast Alaska is one of the few places in the world where, within only a few miles, you can travel from the salt water's edge, through tidal meadows, into temperate rainforest dotted with muskegs, and onto alpine slopes. This rapid transition offers an unusual wealth of habitats to explore, and a great variety of birds to see and hear. Southeast is also on the coastal migration route for many bird species that nest in western and arctic Alaska.

Some 336 species of birds have been documented in Southeast between Dixon Entrance and Yakutat. This is about 70 percent of the birds seen in all of Alaska.

Birds are among the easiest natural creatures to observe. Because of that and our own love of watching birds, this book includes more articles about birds than about any other part of Southeast Alaska's natural world.

There are more bald eagles in Southeast Alaska than anywhere else in the world—an estimated 25,000 of them. Residents and visitors alike seem thrilled to watch them. We've had many personal observations that prompted us to write about bald eagles, but we also had the opportunity to interview Scott Gende, a Juneau ecologist who has climbed to more than 100 nests in the Juneau area to study the importance of food to the success of nesting bald eagles.

Some of our other articles were prompted by our enthusiasm about high quality research we discovered—Bill Calder's work with migrating hummingbirds, Mary Willson and Kim Obermeyer's work on nesting dippers, and Jeff Hughes's work on the importance of old-growth trees to woodpeckers and other cavity-nesting birds.

Sometimes Bob's opportunities to get outstanding photos of birds prompted us to write an article—as in the case of eaglets in the nest, a kingfisher carrying food to its young, a willow ptarmigan on a mountainside in winter plumage, and a yellowlegs screaming at us from a shore pine in the muskeg. In other cases, articles on one subject led us to another. When we wrote about sand lance as "the perfect prey," for example, we started thinking about what might be "the perfect predator," and we came up with an article on owls, which we expanded with Bob's personal recollections.

Our work on "Frequent Fliers" (migrating birds) grew partly out of research Bob was doing to prepare a talk for Migratory Bird Day. What we learned led us to write several articles on shorebirds, which have some of the longest and most interesting migrations of any group of birds.

Lincoln's sparrow

In some instances, we wrote about birds we especially love. Bob particularly likes American dippers because he is fascinated that a songbird can feed underwater, and because he enjoys hearing a dipper's melodious song in the otherwise chilly silence of winter, when no other birds sing. Marge has long been intrigued by the grace and delicacy of herons in flight, and she especially enjoys watching great blues feed along the shore near her cabin on Admiralty Island.

Bob's love of birds led him to devote five years to producing the venerable *Guide to the Birds of Alaska* and to co-authoring with Rich Gordon *A Checklist to the Birds of Southeast Alaska.* Other valuable references include *A Checklist of Alaska Birds,* compiled by Gibson, Heinl, and Tobish, Jr., available for free downloading from the University of Alaska Museum web site; and *A Birder's Guide to Alaska* by George C. West, published by the American Birding Association.

Things
That Go
Squawk
in the Night

Herons often forage for small fish in marshy areas.

You're walking along the beach in Southeast Alaska on a dark night. *Skraawkk!* A raucous shriek splits the air barely 10 feet ahead of you. As you choke down a yelp of surprise, a gravelly *croak! croak! croak!* echoes back from farther and farther away in the darkness. Stop pounding, you tell your heart. The monster is moving *away* from here!

No, you haven't stumbled across an escapee from Jurassic Park, nor a creature from outer space. You've probably disturbed a great blue heron, one of those long-necked, long-legged birds you may have seen in the daytime along a tideflat or perched on a piling or a dock. People in Southeast often see herons, even along roadsides as busy as Egan Drive in Juneau. But many do not know that herons are also active at night.

Herons have a high number of rods—nerve cells highly sensitive to dim light—in their eyes, apparently enabling them to see at night. That is when small fish such as sculpins emerge from under rocks to forage in shallow water. Night-feeding herons are often there to meet them.

Great blue herons are found all over North America, but herons in the Pacific Northwest and Southeast Alaska have darker plumage than birds in other parts of the United States and Canada. Scientists presently classify them as a separate subspecies, *Ardea herodias fannini*. They breed only as far north as Prince William Sound.

We could not find any research conducted on great blue herons in Southeast Alaska, but a great deal of work has been done in British Columbia, and much of it should apply to Southeast. The best work we found was by Robert W. Butler of the Canadian Wildlife Service, who wrote *The Great Blue Heron* (University of British Columbia Press, 1997) and the great blue heron monograph in the definitive series *The Birds of North America* published by the American Ornithological Union.

People seem to enjoy seeing herons—even people who are not otherwise particularly interested in birds. Perhaps they enjoy the glimpse of a long-legged predator unexpectedly wading along a roadside slough. Perhaps they have watched the great, gangly birds lift off and flap gracefully across a sunset sky. Perhaps they have laughed at the

> **"Studying great blues feeding is a good way to get bored out of your gourd . . ."**

comical sight of a scowling, sharp-beaked heap of feathers precariously perched on a rotten piling.

But what else do we know about these lanky Southeast residents?

How they fly

Adult great blue herons have wingspans of about six feet—greater than the reach of many adult humans with their arms outstretched, and nearly as great as the wingspans of bald eagles and trumpeter swans. Because their wing area is large in comparison to their weight, herons lift off the ground easily and fly with deep, slow wingbeats.

A heron's flight exudes utter confidence and ease—*flap . . . flap . . . flap . . .* two to three beats per second—and it ends with a gentle landing, probably meticulously controlled to protect the bird's long, slender legs from the shock of striking hard ground.

Herons have a distinctive profile when they fly, too. Their necks form a characteristic S-shape unlike that of any other Southeast bird, and their legs dangle straight out behind their bodies as if perhaps they're just tagging along for the ride.

Where they're found

We may see herons most frequently near fresh or salt water, but they also turn up in unexpected places. Like eagles, they feed mostly on fish along the shore but nest and roost in large trees. One wonders how they manage to maneuver their broad wings and long legs to get there, but they often perch in spruce or hemlock trees amid thick clusters of branches, where you may see them rocking back and forth to keep their balance like inexperienced high wire artists.

Some herons forage on dry land for small mammals. At Snettisham we watched one pad across more than 300 feet of dry

gravel near the housing units, possibly looking for mice or voles. Ultimately it flapped off and landed in a tall hemlock overlooking Speel River.

How they eat

In Southeast Alaska great blue herons eat mostly small fish. They stalk their prey by standing motionless peering into the water for many minutes, or wading carefully through the shallows, placing each foot gently and deliberately, and spreading their long toes for support. Once a heron, its neck outstretched and its bill pointed downward, sees a fish, it keeps its gaze riveted on the prey. Slowly moving its body forward and under its head, it curves its neck and prepares to strike. *Zap!* The head darts forward as the bird snatches the prey, capturing it between the two serrated parts of the bill as if in a giant—and lethal—pair of tweezers.

Often the heron flips the fish around, shaking it and turning it to slide lengthwise down its throat, or perhaps dropping it on the ground and stabbing it to subdue it.

Staghorn sculpins present special problems because they have sharp, antler-like spines along the sides of their head. (These are in addition to the spines in their first dorsal fin.) Swallowed the wrong way, a sculpin

Because their wing area is large in comparison to their weight, herons lift off the ground easily and fly with deep, slow wingbeats.

Though they may look uncomfortable to us, herons often perch or roost in trees like this hemlock.

can stick in a bird's throat, and occasionally herons die this way. Successful birds drop the sculpins on the ground and stab or peck at them again and again until the spines are relaxed. Only then do they swallow them.

Catching fish is hard work, especially in winter when fish are less plentiful. It's not uncommon for a heron to stalk for 20 minutes or more before catching a meal. James Kushland, a researcher on the East Coast, wrote, "Studying great blues feeding is a good way to get bored out of your gourd, because mostly they just sit there." Still, herons fishing on a low tide beach as the late evening sun dips behind the mountains convey a sense of elegance and well-being that adds special charm to the end of a long summer day.

How they nest

We may see herons often when they're feeding, but seeing them nesting is another story. In some parts of North America the birds nest in large colonies, and their rookeries are readily seen, heard, and . . . *um*, smelled. In fact, there has been a large rookery in Stanley Park in Vancouver, B.C. since at least 1921. But nesting herons are typically extremely secretive and shy. This may be particularly so in Southeast Alaska, where if they nest in colonies at all the number of nests in a colony is probably very small.

Around Juneau we know of nests above Sandy Beach, above Sheep Creek, near Fritz Cove, and above the eel grass bed near the ferry terminal. But even long-time bird-

What Herons Eat

In one study in British Columbia, great blue herons fed mostly on gunnels, eel-like fishes with long, compressed bodies. In another they ate primarily starry flounder, three-spined sticklebacks, and staghorn sculpins.

All these species are commonly found in shallow waters in Southeast Alaska.

starry flounder

staghorn sculpin

three-spined stickleback

crescent gunnel

20

watchers could not tell us of many nests in other areas. That may be just as well, since herons are often susceptible to disturbance when they are nesting. Perhaps they are especially secretive in Southeast, where bald eagles, the major predators on heron young, are so numerous.

Ironically, great blue herons have a great deal in common with bald eagles. Both herons and bald eagles are year-round residents of Southeast. Both feed mostly on fish. Both build large, bulky nests out of sticks placed high in coniferous trees. Males and females of both species share in nest building, incubating, and feeding the young. Both species incubate their eggs for about a month, and both care for their chicks for about two months until the chicks are ready to fly.

Both herons and bald eagles may reuse the same nests for many years, but eagles usually build obvious structures in old-growth trees, while herons often build inconspicuous nests in dense stands of trees that may be second growth.

How they raise their young

Great blue herons usually breed after their second spring. They are generally

monogamous for the length of the season, but they choose new mates each year; and male herons are known to display and lure female herons into mating when their mates are away from the nest.

Herons in Southeast probably begin nesting in late April and normally lay from three to six eggs. Only half the young that are hatched are likely to survive to leave the nest. If the adults flush from the nest, as they are likely to do if disturbed, ravens may swoop in and steal the unprotected eggs, or bald eagles may take the unprotected young.

Catching enough small fish to keep the young fed is a daunting undertaking for both parents. At first the chicks eat regurgitated food, but later they swallow fish directly from the mouth of the parent. One study found that nesting herons fed their two-day-old chicks 10 times in 13 hours. According to another study, a one-month-old chick consumed about the same amount of energy as an average adult heron.

By two months of age young herons are as large as their parents and are ready to fly. Once they leave the nest they are on their own, and they face pretty tough odds. Only about half of them survive.

Young herons of this size eat about the same amount of food as their parents.

Some herons and other large birds lift their wings to shade reflection from the water, but this heron is preening.

On the beach their parents do not feed them or defend them from approaching danger. Only if they learn to take flight early will they escape a bald eagle intent on mak-

Many great blue herons stay in Southeast Alaska all winter. Is this one contemplating its future, or is it thinking, "Perhaps I should have migrated"?

> **Ironically, great blue herons and bald eagles have a great deal in common.**

ing them a meal. Only if they are quick, or perhaps lucky, will they learn how to feed themselves adequately. According to one study, young herons struck at fish at about the same rate as adults, but their capture rate was about half that of adults during their first two months after leaving the nest.

Herons fledged early in the summer have an advantage because they learn to feed when fish are more plentiful. If they are fortunate, they may live for another 20 years.

Their future in Southeast

Heron populations are declining and have been officially declared "vulnerable" in British Columbia, where population growth and urban expansion have taken over much of the coastal and forest land the birds used to use.

Robert Butler estimates there may be only about 300 nesting pairs of herons along the Alaska coastline. Whether they survive will depend on whether there are safe places for them to nest, habitat in which they can feed, and large enough populations of small fish available to sustain them.●

To Mexico and Back Again

Southeast's Smallest Migrants

In early summer in Southeast Alaska, one of the great pleasures for residents is keeping bright red sugar-water feeders filled with nectar to feed rufous hummingbirds. Buzzing and sparring, glinting in shades of red-brown and metallic green, the birds often jockey noisily with each other for the chance to sip their next meal. They seem like tiny miracles—and indeed they are. They have traveled thousands of miles from their wintering grounds in Mexico to nest in Southeast Alaska.

Hummingbirds begin arriving in early to mid- April, but by late June the males will be on their way south again. Females and young of the year will leave in mid-July/early August. All the birds will travel 1,700 to 2,700 miles to reach their wintering grounds by September.

What routes do they follow? Where do they stop to refuel? What affects their ability to survive the long journey?

Tracking birds as small as hummingbirds to answer such questions is difficult. But some insights have come from the work of Bill Calder, a researcher and professor at the University of Arizona, who studied rufous hummingbirds for more than 30 years.

Calder found that hummingbirds stop to refuel in high mountain meadows just as certain alpine and subalpine flowers are at the peak of blooming. In July and August some appear in meadows of the Coast and Sierra Mountains at elevations of 5,500 to 7,000 feet, perhaps visiting the same patches of flowers they visited during past fall migrations. Others turn up in the Rocky Mountains, where summer flowers typically reach their prime during the monsoons.

That birds so small have journeyed even this far is quite remarkable. In fact, Calder likes to calculate their trips in hummingbird body lengths—which total almost 49 million, the longest migration of any bird by such a standard.

Adult male hummingbirds have brilliant red "gorgets" (throat feathers). Tiny barbules on the feathers reflect increased light at certain angles, so the bird's gorget seems to flash brilliant color as it moves about.

In early spring rufous hummingbirds leave their wintering grounds in Mexico and head north to nest and raise their young. Traveling up the west coast of North America, some turn inland toward Idaho, Montana, and Alberta, Canada. Others continue north to British Columbia and coastal Alaska as far north as Prince William Sound.

In mid-July and August, first the males then the females and young of the year fly south. Some travel along the Coast Range and the Sierra Nevadas. Others travel farther east along the Rocky Mountains.

Most hummingbirds from Southeast Alaska probably follow the Coast Range/Sierra Nevada route.

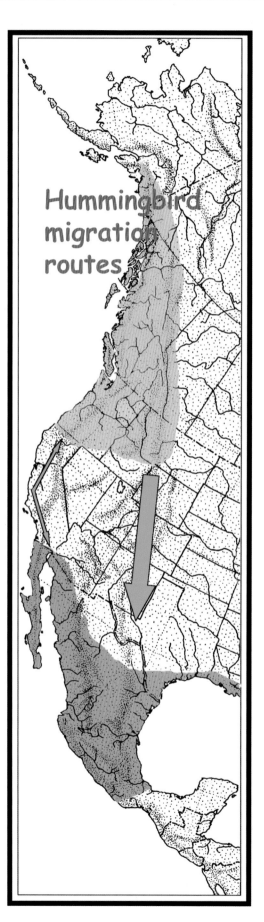

Hummingbird migration routes

Calder wrote in the book *Gatherings of Angels—Migrating Birds and Their Ecology:*

> *Small size is . . . a disadvantage for seasonal home-changing. Small size puts limits on fat storage and flight speed, and that reduces endurance and range between refuelings. A Canada goose, for example, can fly six times as far between fueling stops, at two or three times the hummingbird's 25-mph speed (no tail wind). . . . If the fuel supply runs short, the weather changes, or the migrating hummingbird is blown off course or forced down unexpectedly, the unlucky bird might be far from a flowering meadow.*

In situations such as these it may be difficult, or impossible, for the bird to recover enough to continue its journey.

"Social" birds like Canada geese have other advantages, Calder said. Geese pool their experience and route knowledge with flock mates and relatives, and they reduce energy costs by flying in V-formation. "Anti-social" hummingbirds lack these advantages, because they develop no social ties, even at

Hummingbirds stop to refuel in high mountain meadows.

the family level. Each bird is on its own.

And what about the young of the year? How do juvenile hummingbirds—barely a month out of the nest—manage this long, dangerous migration? Calder believed instructions for the migratory flight must be encoded in the genes. Juvenile birds get no guidance from their parents on migration routes. By the time they begin to head south their parents have already left.

In preparation for only one leg of the trip to Mexico, hummingbirds may increase their body weight by two-thirds. Calder writes, "Once fully-fattened, a hummingbird the size of a rufous could fly an estimated 610 miles of its migration route without refueling. With a tail wind it could fly even farther."

> "Once fully fattened, a hummingbird the size of a rufous could fly an estimated 610 miles of its migration route without refueling."

But refueling stops are crucial, and Calder notes that "timing and amount of precipitation must often determine the success of migratory nectar-feeders. If there is summer drought, so that seasonal flowers die or wither, birds face tremendous competition for nectar sources, and they may be unable to refuel successfully. Describing his observations of just such a situation in 1996 and 1997, Calder wrote, "Two consecutive years is long enough for a generation of hummingbirds to have died, and such sustained climatic vicissitudes, if widespread, could have a significant impact on the species' population."

While habitat protection is important, he noted, "the greatest vulnerability may come from the effects of climate change."

Here is a theme that keeps repeating itself as we learn about many species of migratory birds: Everything is connected. And events far from us can tremendously affect the birds we enjoy no matter where we live. It's a story borne out by Southeast's smallest migrants, and perhaps those most widely anticipated each spring. ●

(Above left) Hummingbirds are attracted to several species of paintbrush, some of which are quite common in Southeast Alaska meadows.

(Above right) Western columbine flowers have evolved specifically to attract hummingbirds, rather than bees or other insects, as pollinators. They are usually bright red or orange, colors conspicuous to hummingbirds but not to bees.

Learning about hummingbirds

Most of what we know about hummingbirds has come from the dedicated and painstaking work of Bill Calder, who researched hummingbirds for 30 years before his death in April 2002. For several years Bill and his wife Lorene came to Southeast Alaska to study and band rufous hummingbirds. One of their regular stops was Bob Armstrong's back porch in Juneau.

Each hummingbird Bill caught he weighed, banded, and examined for fat content and a characteristic pattern of wear on the tail feathers that would indicate it was feeding nestlings. He also removed a tail feather for later DNA analysis.

Rufous hummingbirds are very docile and do not put up a struggle when they're

handled. The female in the photo above laid quietly in Bill's hand until he gave it a gentle nudge and it buzzed off.

You can see the numbered aluminum leg band and the temporary blue mark Bill used to distinguish birds that had been recently handled.

Alaska's

State Bird

It might have been the robin, or the raven, or the snowy owl. But after 6,000 school children finished voting in the mid-1950s, the willow ptarmigan was destined to bear the title of Alaska's State Bird.

The students' choice was sent to the Territorial Legislature and then to the Governor. Signing the "Act to name an official bird" on February 4, 1955, Territorial Governor B. Frank Heintzleman wrote:

The Willow Ptarmigan has a number of qualities which recommend it for this signal honor. It is found in all parts of Alaska and is widely known and easily recognized. It does not fly south in the fall as do most of the ducks, geese, swans and song birds, but spends its entire life in the Territory.

All three species of ptarmigan—the rock, the white-tailed, and the willow—are found in Southeast Alaska. In spring and summer, if you're hiking in the alpine, rock ptarmigan are the species you'll most often run into. White-tailed ptarmigan generally stay on the highest peaks and ridges.

Willow ptarmigan frequent brushy areas, especially near treeline. They favor moist areas with well-drained soil, where low-growing willows provide fuzzy catkins, buds, leaves, and twigs for food depending on the season.

In winter, all three species move to lower elevations, where the shrubs they feed on may be more exposed. If you see a ptarmigan at sea level in winter, it's usually a willow.

Ptarmigan are indeed widely known in Alaska. They were long an important food source in virtually all our Native cultures, and are taken now by sportsmen and subsistence hunters alike. In 1954-57, the Alaska Department of Fish and Game estimated 50,000 ptarmigan a year were harvested by hunters from 61 villages, and that was during a period when ptarmigan populations were low.

Ptarmigan are also an important food source for other animals, particularly in winter, when other foods are not available. In Southeast Alaska, willow ptarmigan may be taken by hawks, falcons, and bald or golden eagles. Eggs and young also are particularly vulnerable to wolves and ravens.

Ptarmigan do stay in Alaska year-round, and the remarkable adaptations they have developed for winter are well known among Alaskans. Each fall, feather density increases all over their bodies, and they develop "snowshoes"—dense feathers on the top and bottom of each foot—that help them move about in deep snow. The claws on their feet also elongate, effectively giving them built-in "crampons" for walking on icy surfaces. Even in their digestive system special bacteria develop to help them break down the woody twigs and buds they rely on for food in winter.

Like good Alaskans, ptarmigan have also learned to hunker down and wait out winter weather. When temperatures drop they may spend as much as 80 percent of their time burrowed beneath the snow, where ambient temperatures are generally higher and they are protected from the wind. If the snow becomes icy and this shelter is not available, many birds may die.

Willow ptarmigan have one other characteristic that Governor Heintzleman may well have praised if he had known about it. Unlike any other members of the grouse/ptarmigan family, male willow ptarmigan are extremely attentive parents. If the female is killed after the eggs have hatched, the male will raise the chicks to independence.

Males stay with their mates throughout the nesting period. They protect the female from other males, and usually perch close by her, keeping watch for predators. If hikers or potential predators approach, the male

(Preceding page) Willow buds, twigs, leaves, and catkins are a very large part of the willow ptarmigan's diet in all seasons. The spring catkins this male is eating are particularly high in protein.

Dressing for the Season

In spring and summer, female willow ptarmigan (above) are brownish with yellowish barring on their underparts—a coloration that helps camouflage them from predators once the snow has melted from their high elevation range.

As in the title page photo for this article, male willow ptarmigan change from winter white to cryptic summer plumage more slowly than females do. In spring and early summer their handsome reddish brown head, neck, and chest feathers contrast strikingly with the white winter plumage on the rest of their bodies.

The more gradual change from winter plumage in males may benefit females and young birds by making males more visible to predators, or it may help signal their presence to any other males that might disrupt the family situation.

The red comb seen on the spring male can be inflated to attract females during breeding season. Note the "snowshoes" and "crampons" on the feet of the white-plumaged winter bird, above.

will sound an alarm call (a kind of growling *to-BAK-a, to-BAK-a, to-BAK-a*), then will fly or run to lead the predators away.

Some males are very protective. One summer we saw a male willow ptarmigan land on the back of a northern harrier and successfully drive it away when it approached an apparent nesting area. We have also heard reports of willow ptarmigan attacking humans and even bears.

Certainly the winter wren, the snow bunting, or the Steller's jay would have had wonderful qualities to recommend them as one of Alaska's official symbols. But as Governor Heintzleman wrote:

The school children of Alaska have shown a great interest in selecting an official bird. . . . Both houses of the Legislature voted unanimously in passing the present bill. . . . For these compelling reasons, therefore, I am today signing House Bill No. 2 of the 22nd Alaska Legislature, and 90 days from this date the Willow Ptarmigan will become the official bird of the Territory of Alaska and entitled to all the prerogatives, pleasures and advantages of that designation.

We do wonder, though, what those "prerogatives, pleasures and advantages" might be from the willow ptarmigan's perspective! ●

Eagle
Acrobatics

If you spend much time on or near the water in Southeast you've probably been lucky enough to watch a bald eagle catch a fish. What a thrill! Suddenly a magnificent bird with a six- to eight-foot wing span glides down over the water, stabs its yellow feet toward the water's surface, and—incredibly!—flies off with the prize.

How do eagles do it? The following photos capture the sequence. The accompanying "Recollections" tell how the photos were taken.●

1) *From their perches in tall conifers, eagles may watch for hours waiting for fish to float by or swim by near the surface.*

2) *Once a fish is sighted, the eagle launches from its hunting perch.*

Bob's Recollections

One summer in late July and early August I watched and photographed bald eagles catching fish about 25 times between Sheep Creek and Point Bishop, south of Juneau.

I cruised the shoreline by skiff and looked for bald eagles perched near the water's edge and at some distance from their nest site. I then put a Pacific herring or a staghorn sculpin (which I'd partly pumped up with air so they'd float) out in the water

so the tide or wind would carry the fish about 50 to 100 feet in front of the shoreline where the eagle was perched. Then I slowly backed the skiff away and attempted to stay about 100 feet from where the fish was floating.

Most eagles sighted the fish within five minutes after I'd placed it on the water, and most of them went after it within 10 minutes after I'd set it afloat. A few times a gull was attracted to the fish,   →

3) A high glide carries the eagle toward the fish, usually at 100 to 200 feet elevation.

4) A side-slip causes the eagle to begin losing altitude.

5) With its wings slightly folded, the eagle swoops rapidly toward the water.

but as soon as it circled over or landed near the fish, the eagle would lift off from its perch and scare it away.

One time, just after I'd placed the fish in the water, I heard a sound like a jet plane and looked up just as an eagle swooped down from its perch and snatched the fish up within 10 feet of the boat. I was really startled!

Most of the eagles I observed followed a similar pattern. They usually started with a high glide off the perch tree, from about 100 to 200 feet elevation, made a side-slip in which they turned nearly upside down, and then swooped to descend rapidly to within two feet of the water's surface.

During the descent, their legs were extended and their talons were closed like a fist. Then just as they were ready to strike, the birds would raise their legs, open their talons, and thrust their legs downward to snatch the fish. →

6) The eagle glides swiftly along the water's surface.

7) As it nears striking distance, the eagle's legs and feet push forward. It opens its talons and raises its wings.

Up until they got the fish, the eagles didn't flap their wings at all, and for that whole time—and sometimes immediately after—the birds fixed their eyes intently on the fish.

Once the fish was in their talons, the eagles raised their wings high and began flapping to regain altitude.

In all the incidents I observed the sun was at the birds' backs. Perhaps that is yet one more factor in the success of these precise maneuvers.

After capturing a Pacific herring, most eagles took the fish immediately to the nest. If they caught a staghorn sculpin, they usually took it to a rock along the shoreline that was fairly protected from above. There they tore it apart and ate it, then either flew to their nest or flew to a perch and resumed hunting.

My presence did not seem to interfere with the eagles' behavior. Since the eagles would be feeding what they caught to their young, I also checked with the Tom Brown bait company to be sure the →

8) Success! The eagle has snatched the fish from the water and begins flapping its wings to regain altitude.

9) Only mature eagles seem to be skilled enough to catch fish from the surface of the water. A mature eagle can probably carry a fish weighing about five to six pounds.

herring did not contain any additives or contaminants. They assured me it contained no additives and came from a relatively pristine bay off British Columbia.

I suspect it takes eagles several years of practice to perfect their hunting skills. In the beginning some of the eagles I presented fish to were in immature plumage, but I never saw one of them succeed in taking a fish. They seemed inept and would often attempt to snatch with their feet when they were too high above the water's surface.

Even among eagles in mature plumage, some were more adept than others, as if they'd had a little more practice in aerial acrobatics. ●

Raising an Eaglet

Peep . . . peep . . . peep. The faint, high-pitched sound is coming from one of two dull white eggs lying in the center of a gigantic jumble of sticks near the top of a large spruce tree. The eggs lie in a small depression lined with soft moss and grass. Crouched just above them, a female bald eagle shelters them with her body, her wings slightly opened. It is enough to shield them from the chilly spring breeze that blows in from the salt water nearby.

The egg "peeps" again, wiggling and jerking as the tiny eaglet inside pecks at the shell. It is hammering with a small bony "egg tooth" on the top of its beak. Soon a crack and then a small hole appear in the egg. A few hours later, the eaglet emerges, wet and bedraggled in a coat of pale gray down.

The newly hatched eaglet is totally helpless. Her eyes are not open. She can barely move around, and she cannot feed herself. She will not be able to maintain her body temperature for several weeks. Right now she weighs about three ounces, but in three months she could well weigh 40 or 50 times that much.

According to Mark V. Stalmaster, author of the fascinating book *The Bald Eagle*, she may eventually gain up to 6.3 ounces a day. That is the fastest growth rate of any North American bird.

Responsibilities of Parenthood

Raising young eaglets and preparing for them is a tremendous investment for bald

This eaglet hatched about May 22 and is in its secondary down plumage. The photo was taken on June 14.

Parents of the eaglet shown on the preceding page. "Mom" is on the right, "Pop" on the left. Eagle parents devote about six months to raising their young.

eagle parents. It means about six months of hard work and staying almost constantly within a limited nesting territory.

If a female bald eagle has survived the winter in good condition, and if she and her mate have successfully built a nest together, she will lay one or more eggs (in most cases, two) in late April or early May.

For the next 35 days the female and her mate must incubate the eggs, keeping them warm, protecting them from predators such as crows or ravens, and turning them approximately every hour to keep them evenly warm and prevent the membranes of the embryos inside from sticking to the shells.

The male does not feed the female during this time, as some birds do. Instead, he forages to feed himself while the female is on the nest, then returns to relieve her so she can fly off and eat.

Even before the eggs hatch, eagle parents begin gathering food for their young. Perhaps alerted by the peeping sound as young eaglets work to break out of their shells, the adults begin caching food in the nest. They bring small fish—maybe herring or sand lance—and larger ones—a walleye pollock, perhaps—providing the same amount of food they will provide when the nestlings are older, as if to be sure there will be enough.

When the eaglets are young, the parents must tear the food into tiny bits, dangling it from their bills so the hungry chicks will gobble it down. As the eaglets get older, they may squeal and scream for food, grabbing at their parents' bills, shoving and pecking at each other, and snatching sometimes enormous chunks of fish and gulping them down.

Nesting eagles usually bring food to their young at least once every few hours, and they will need to do so for some 11 to 12 weeks until the eaglets fledge and leave the nest.

The Challenge of Getting a Meal

Nesting eagles stay close to their nest sites—usually within about one square mile. Typically they perch on tall trees or snags where they can see large areas of water—and that is how we often see them, their white heads clearly visible against the dark green forest behind them. From their perches the birds may wait for hours for fish to swim by near the water's surface, or for dead or dying fish to float by or wash up on the beach. Eagles have incredibly powerful eyesight. We've seen them spot fish and zero in on them from thousands of feet away.

But obtaining fish from the water is no easy task. Watching a bald eagle swoop down from its perch, snatch a large fish from the water, and grandly carry it to a waterside perch is one of the more exciting events Southeast residents and visitors are sometimes privileged to enjoy.

We have watched very carefully to see exactly how eagles perform this difficult feat. We saw that some eagles are better at it than others, and we never saw an immature eagle succeed at it. (The immatures nearly always missed their mark by a considerable distance and usually ended up grabbing talonsful of air several feet above the water.) We believe it must take eagles years of practice to perfect this hunting technique.

Eagles may also pirate their meals from others. We've seen eagles steal fish from river otters, ospreys, mergansers, gulls, and of course each other. Several times we have seen an otter catch a flounder or a sculpin, then swim ashore to eat it. As the otter tore the fish apart for its meal, a bald eagle swooped down at it with such speed and surprise the otter dropped the fish and fell backwards into the water, while the eagle—still airborne—grabbed the fish and flew off with it.

Eagles also take fish injured by whales and sea lions, or driven to the surface by loons, seals, or salmon. Several times we have watched eagles follow feeding marbled murrelets, swoop to the water's surface, and emerge with talonsful of sand lance that the murrelets had driven up from deeper water. More than once we've seen an eagle swoop down and steal a small duck shortly after it had been taken on the tidal flats by a northern harrier.

Southeast Alaska's widespread commercial, sport, and subsistence fisheries must provide a considerable number of fish carcasses that eagles can pick up for food. Most fishing in Southeast takes place from May through August, the time when bald eagles are nesting and gathering food for their nestlings.

Fish that are injured and thrown back into the water often swim about at the sur-

Beginning in July carcasses of spawning salmon become important food for eagle parents. For newly fledged juvenile eagles, salmon carcasses are probably the most important food available.

37

On July 9, three and a half weeks after the first photo in this article was taken, the same eaglet now has a complete set of juvenile feathers. Despite its size, it will still need several weeks of care and feeding by the adults. It was spotted flying from the nest in mid-August.

face, where eagles could reach them. Fish that die usually sink to the bottom, beyond reach; but members of the cod family, such as walleye pollock, float because their gas bladder expands when they are pulled up quickly from deep water.

When researchers studied the stomach contents of some 325 nesting eagles (birds killed under Alaska's predator control program, in effect from 1917 to 1952), they found pollock and cod in about a third of them. They also found that pollock were the most frequently consumed fish during May and June before salmon spawning began and during a critical time for eagles nesting and raising young.

Care Until Eaglets Leave the Nest

Besides feeding their youngsters several times a day, eagle parents also must "brood" them, or keep them warm. Even though they go through two different plumages of downy feathers, eaglets are unable to keep

themselves warm for a number of weeks.

For the first month, one or the other parent is seldom away from the nest. Once nestlings are about a month old, they begin sprouting flight and contour feathers amid their down, but still the parents must protect them if there is rain, wind, or too much sun.

When the parents are away from the nest, older eaglets seem to prepare for their adult life by playing. They may flap their wings, jump around in the nest, fight with one another, or play tug of war with sticks. Some eaglets are so aggressive they attack their parents when the adults bring food to the nest; in that case, the parents just fly by the nest and drop food off, faithful to their duties but unwilling to put up with their offspring!

Once eaglets have developed most of their wing and tail feathers (usually when they're 11 to 12 weeks old), they are ready to fledge, or leave the nest. Some leave on their own. Others need to be lured away, perhaps by a parent flying overhead with food and calling to them.

In *The Bald Eagle* Stalmaster estimates that perhaps half of all fledglings fall to the ground after their first flight. Whether they fall or successfully land in trees near the nest, the parents will often, but not always, bring them food. Some studies found that most fledglings stayed within a mile of the nest for six to eight weeks, and some eaglets returned to the nest to pick up food their parents had cached.

We can hardly overstate the value of spawned out salmon to juvenile eagles that have left the nest but are not yet very skilled at hunting. Juvenile eagles are probably very much dependent for their survival on salmon carcasses washed up on beaches or river banks, or dragged to shore and abandoned by bears.

As winter approaches, juvenile eagles tend to travel more widely than adults. Some young eagles travel as far south as British Columbia or Washington state in search of accessible food. Meanwhile their parents—relieved at last from their tremendous responsibilities—are free to forage beyond their nesting territories, perhaps even traveling to winter feeding grounds such as the Chilkat Valley near Haines. Those that are likely to nest again the next year, however, may remain near their territory or occasionally return to assert ownership throughout the winter. ⬢

Timeline for Raising an Eaglet

This chart, based on work by Juneau ecologist Scott Gende, shows the timing of egg laying, hatching, and rearing of eaglets at nests in the Juneau area.

Most eaglets, like the one shown in the photo, are ready to leave the nest by mid-August.

April	May	June	July	August
	P E A K	P E A K	Nestling period	

Laying dates   Hatching dates

The Key to Nesting Success

When Scott Gende, an ecologist with the Pacific Northwest Research Station in Juneau, studied nesting eagles in the Juneau area, he found that once eaglets hatched, their parents were usually successful at raising them to leave the nest as fledglings. But among in their nest even while the eggs are still incubating. In the more than 100 nests he visited Gende found a variety of fish cached: Pacific herring, Pacific sand lance, eulachon, walleye pollock, sculpins, flounders, rockfish, Dolly Varden, and pink salmon.

This photo shows prey cached at one nest Scott Gende climbed to in May, just after the eaglets had hatched. Note the two eaglets huddled together to the right.

Pacific herring

Walleye pollock

Eaglets

Scott Gende

the nests that failed to produce fledglings, 95 percent failed during the incubation period.

Gende believes this indicates how crucial it is that eagle parents find adequate food during the early weeks when they are incubating their eggs.

He found the most successful bald eagle nests were those located where fish could be obtained most easily in April and May—near areas, for example, where herring spawn. But even if food is nearby, eagle parents also have to be skilled enough at hunting to get it, and they have to work together to keep their eggs constantly covered while they each still manage to get enough to eat.

Bald eagles cache food for the young

The kinds of fish depended on what was available at particular times of the year. Gende found herring and eulachon in nests during April and May, when these fish spawn in shallow water. He found walleye pollock most often at nests located along deep-water shorelines where these fish reside.

In July, pink salmon were often the only species cached in nests. (Early July is when pink salmon begin congregating in large schools near shore before they enter streams to spawn.) In a few cases, Gende found carcasses or remnants of birds cached at eagle nests, including the remains of crows, two white-winged scoters, and one raven.

King *of* Fishers

This female kingfisher has captured a young salmon to feed to its nestlings.

Southeast Alaska has more than its share of good fishermen, human and otherwise. And one of the best is the belted kingfisher.

We usually hear kingfishers before we see them. Walking along a stream or a saltwater beach, you might be startled by a loud, prolonged chattering as a kingfisher flies by, giving its characteristic "rattle call."

Kingfishers call at the slightest disturbance, vigorously defending their feeding territory at all times of the year. One might even land on a branch in front of you and continue rattling even while it is carrying a fish in its beak.

Belted kingfishers feed almost exclusively on small fish about three to four inches long. They catch them in clear, open water, usually no more than two feet deep. Generally, they eat whatever species are most available, including staghorn sculpins, tidepool sculpins, gunnels, three-spined sticklebacks, young Dolly Varden, and fingerlings of various species of salmon.

Belted kingfishers are one of the few North American birds in which the female is more colorful than the male. Both males and females have stocky bodies, gray backs, and a white collar around the neck. Males have a single gray band across their white belly. Females have the same band but also rufous sides and a rufous band across the lower breast. Both males and females have shaggy crests, tufts of feathers on the tops of their heads, which they raise and lower depending on their mood.

During nesting the male must feed the female for about three weeks.

It can be a tremendous pleasure to sit and watch a kingfisher fish. Watching from its perch, a few feet or more above the water, the bird will suddenly dive into the water

A Kingfisher's Successful Dive

1) The kingfisher folds its wings back and dives like an arrow into the water.

2) This time it completely submerges in pursuit of its prey.

3) It leaves the water in full flight carrying what might be a sculpin.

head first and, if it's lucky, come up carrying a small fish. Typically the bird will then fly to a perch and pound its prize against the perch with sideways movements of its head. (This stuns or kills the fish, and breaks the spines if it is a stickleback or staghorn sculpin.) It will then swallow its meal head-first.

Kingfishers had best be good fishers. During nesting the male must feed the female for about three weeks, beginning approximately 10 days before she lays the first egg. During the following 22 days, the male shares care of the eggs, and once the eggs are hatched both parents begin feeding the young.

Belted kingfishers usually lay six to seven eggs, and once the young birds hatch, parents must feed them for about three weeks. Biologist William James Davis, who studied belted kingfishers in Ohio, estimated that parent birds make some 1,200 trips carrying food to the nest over that three-week period. Davis estimated that, with six to eight chicks to feed, parents with nearly grown young needed to catch 90 fish a day to feed themselves and their offspring. If heavy rains or storms disrupt water clarity in the area where the parents fish, catching that many fish can be difficult. If they're not fed adequately, nestlings can starve to death.

This male kingfisher is carrying a staghorn sculpin to its nest in a sandy bank.

Kingfisher nestlings are capable of digesting the bones and scales of fish, but once they get older they lose this ability, perhaps because their gastric juices change from acid to alkaline. Adult kingfishers disgorge compact little pellets containing scales and bones of fish they have eaten. Studies

Parents teach their young to fish for themselves.

of these pellets, often found beneath a frequently used perch, have helped researchers determine what species of fish kingfishers eat and even the ages of the fish.

Once young kingfishers are ready to fly, their parents will lure them from the nest by dropping fish outside the nest or calling from perches near the entrance. During

the next three weeks, the parents teach the young to fish for themselves. They usually accomplish this task by refusing to feed the youngsters. Instead they drop stunned fish into the water until the young fly down to retrieve them. Once the young can catch live fish on their own, a process that usually takes about 10 days, the parents drive them away from their home territory.

During his research in Ohio, William James Davis found that less than half a kingfisher's dives were successful. He estimated a success rate of 44 percent at the very best fishing holes. That percentage represents tremendous effort in relation to final results for these avian fishers; but translated into catch per rod hours, they'd be enough to please many human fishers in Southeast waters.●

Crazy Corvids

Ravens, crows, Steller's jays, and magpies. You can hardly get through a day in Southeast without encountering at least one of these feathered hooligans. Corvids such as these—members of the family *Corvidae*—are generally gregarious, aggressive, and very vocal. They adapt well to the presence of humans, and may also be among the most intelligent of animals.

Black-billed magpie

Northwestern crow

Over the years, we've had a number of unusual experiences with ravens and other corvids. Here are some of the more memorable stories—tales that we feel easily earn these birds the nickname "Crazy Corvids."

Steller's jay

Common raven

An Album of Corvids

(Right) Ravens that often feed on barnacles have worn places in their beaks. In this photo you can see through the worn beak to the water in the background.

(Below) It's fun to listen to the romantic burblings of paired ravens.

Ravens are wonderful fliers. You see them riding thermals with bald eagles, or doing barrel rolls with each other, or playing in the wind, wingtips curled and tail feathers spread. They are also very vocal. R.N. Brown, a graduate student at the University of Alaska Fairbanks, described more than 30 different kinds of raven calls. They ranged from the *Kaaa* call to a deep resonant *Quork, Quork, Quork*, a melodious warbling, and a loud, high-pitched yell.

Ravens begin courting in Southeast as early as January, and they sometimes engage in intriguing behaviors. You might see a male raven soaring, wheeling, and tumbling in the sky, or observe a male and a female flying one above the other with their wingtips touching. I've watched the big black birds pass objects to each other in flight; and one day on a mountain ridge near Juneau several hoodlums "played"

Common Raven

with me. Again and again they rode up high on thermals, flipped on their backs just a few feet from my face, and uttered *kukuk* as if it was some kind of communication I should understand.

One of my funniest experiences with ravens was when I saw about seven to nine ravens standing around in a circle at Brotherhood Park in Juneau. One at a time, each of the ravens picked up an object—a piece of Styrofoam®, a hunk of wadded up paper—and walked into the center of the circle. It stopped for a minute as if it was showing what it had to all the rest of the birds in the circle. Then it went back to its spot, and another bird would walk into the middle of the circle with an object.

One raven had a paper cup—a pretty large one, like you would get for a large soft drink. Finally it picked that up and walked into the middle of the circle—and that ended the game! I don't know whether that bird had the "best object" or the "top prize," or what, but after that all the birds flew away.

Northwestern Crow

For awhile a number of crows came often to the deck of my house in Juneau. About six of them became quite tame and would sit along the railing and watch me when I was sitting out on the deck. I started giving them peanuts once in awhile and got the idea of playing the shell game with them. So I got three paper cups and every so often I would put a peanut under one cup and then shuffle the cups around to see if the crows could figure out which one had the peanut under it.

They could!

All the birds would stand on the railing and watch me—They'd watch what cup I put the peanut under—and as I shuffled the cups to different spots, they always seemed to know where the peanut was. Most of them would come over, pick up the cup, set it down, then grab the peanut and fly off with it.

But one of them seemed a little unsure of itself. It knew where the peanut was but didn't seem to know quite what to do. Finally, it came over and picked up the cup, but as it did, another crow edged over, grabbed the peanut, and flew off with the prize. So the timid crow flew off, too—carrying the cup! It was as if the first crow knew he'd lost out and was trying to save face by pretending he knew what he was doing.

I had another odd experience with crows a number of years ago. I was sitting in a blind I'd set up to photograph bald eagles, and there were a number of crows foraging along the beach nearby. Suddenly, the crows started bringing small rocks and piling them in front of the blind. Just one crow at a time would grab a rock off the beach, then walk up and set it very gently in this pile. Pretty soon there was a mound of rocks sitting in front of me about four inches high. Then the crows just left! That was it.

I never did figure out what was going on. I could see no connection between the crows' behavior and anything I had done. All I could think of was that maybe they were "marking" me, the way hikers use cairns to mark a trail.

(Above) One of crows' favorite foods in Southeast is blue mussels, which they often carry aloft and drop to crack open.

(Left) Crows have a variety of vocalizations, including a cat-like mewing that's almost certain to attract human attention.

Steller's Jay

In two different locations—at a fisheries research station where I worked on Admiralty Island and at home here in Juneau—I've had Steller's jays that peer in the window at me and knock on the glass with their beaks to be fed. Here at home, if I don't respond right away, and maybe move to another place in the house, the jay will follow me to the closest window, perch on the window sill, and look in. This bird is very persistent. It doesn't give up until I open the door and throw it a couple of peanuts.

Steller's jays are great imitators. I've seen them swoop into a bird feeder imitating the call of a red-tailed hawk so convincingly that all the other birds will scatter. Once I watched one give a perfect imitation of a calling bald eagle. And another time, on Mount Jumbo, I heard a marmot whistling from the top of a tree, only to find the whistling was coming from a Steller's jay rather than a furry ground-dweller that had somehow mysteriously grown wings.

When you hear jays making a lot of noise in the woods it's always fun to see what they're up to. Sometimes there'll be an owl around. Jays are usually among the first animals to discover bird predators in the forest, and they'll do a lot of talking to them—squawking and making a big hullabaloo. I don't think they're as much into dive bombing predators as crows are.

Black-billed Magpie

Black-billed magpies, which we see in Southeast mostly in the winter, are as bold as the vivid black and white of their plumage. They usually travel in groups like young hoods, and they're often less cautious than ravens about coming directly to food associated with humans.

If you put out table scraps, magpies will swoop down and stuff their beaks with as much as they can carry, then they'll fly off. This sometimes works to the benefit of ravens, who will wait safely in nearby trees, then chase the magpies till they drop the scraps—which the ravens, of course, quickly retrieve.

Magpies are pretty good pirates, too.

Last winter when I was out walking Nola, our lanky black dog, she came across a piece of salmon skin near a spawning stream. She picked it up and started running really fast through the forest. And right on her tail was a magpie, keeping up with her all the way.

It made quite a scene—a thin, lanky black dog running along with a long-tailed white and black bird chasing her. I don't know whether the magpie was after the fish skin or just enjoying the thrill of the race, but they tore off through the woods together, and I'm sure they gave each other a run for their money.

Clark's Nutcracker

A rare visitor to Southeast Alaska, a Clark's nutcracker accepted handouts from a woman in Douglas.

The woman would open her screen door and yell, "Clarkie! Clarkie!" and this crazy corvid would fly out of the forest to accept a peanut from her hand.

49

Sentinels
of the
Bog

Here you are hiking through a gorgeous Southeast Alaska muskeg when suddenly the tranquility of the afternoon is shattered by the incessant screams of a large, long-legged bird perched precariously atop a scraggly shore pine. As you make your way through boggy hummocks and low shrubs, the bird flies from treetop to treetop, following you with a constant ratcheting protest. There may even be two birds, and their calling may be so rapid and intense that you cannot tell the calls apart.

You've no doubt stumbled into a greater yellowlegs nesting area.

We've had the same experience. On Admiralty Island a yellowlegs once chased us through a muskeg for a quarter of a mile. Another time we walked clear across Spaulding Meadows near Juneau and saw three pairs of yellowlegs within about two miles. Each pair screamed and yelped at us and had barely stopped before the next pair began. Basically we were accompanied by yellowlegs the entire trip.

It's unlikely you will ever find the nest a greater yellowlegs is defending. It's not just that the birds' ear-splitting cries make the thought of staying around quite unappealing. It's also that if a bird stays quietly on

> **Greater yellowlegs also act as alert sentinels while they're feeding on tidal flats.**

its nest, it will often not flush until you are only a few feet away. In our many years of tramping around Southeast muskegs and being yelled at by yellowlegs, we have found only one nest. That bird didn't flush until, inadvertently, we were about to step on it.

Greater yellowlegs also act as alert sentinels while they're feeding on tidal flats away

from their nesting territories. In response to intruders they may be the first amongst a mixed flock of shorebirds to sound the alarm; yet, surprisingly, they're usually the last birds to leave.

Greater yellowlegs also differ from other sandpipers in their feeding habits. They are the only sandpipers in Alaska that feed extensively on fish. (Other sandpipers eat mostly insects, small mollusks, and crustaceans.) When they are feeding, yellowlegs can put on quite a show. We've often watched them walk along or run in water just a few inches deep, then suddenly lunge, often submerging their heads and emerging with a small fish sideways in their bill.

In Southeast we believe they eat mostly three-spined sticklebacks and young staghorn sculpins—no mean feat when you consider the defenses both these species of little fish have. Staghorn sculpins have sharp, antler-like spines along the sides of

Greater yellowlegs are the noisiest shorebirds in Southeast Alaska. If you encounter one in a muskeg near its nest it will screech at you without letup until you leave the area.

Greater yellowlegs chicks are "precocial." They will leave their nest within 24 hours after the last of their clutch has hatched and begin to feed themselves.

their head, and spines in their first dorsal fin. Swallowed the wrong way, they could stick in a bird's throat.

Three-spined sticklebacks also have sharp spines—three on their back and one on each side of the belly. All the spines can lock open or outward. So they, too, could be difficult for a predator to swallow.

Yellowlegs seem to overcome these defenses by grabbing the fish with their long bills, dropping then picking them up several times, and otherwise manipulating them for some moments before swallowing them whole, headfirst. Perhaps this handling allows the yellowlegs to position the fish in just the right way so they can be easily swallowed, or it causes the spines to relax so the fish don't get caught in the yellowlegs' throat.

You may see greater yellowlegs in Southeast Alaska between April and October. They are one of the last sandpipers to leave Southeast in the fall, and by winter both adults and juveniles will have traveled to central California, Mexico, or as far south as Tierra del Fuego. They'll be one of the first shorebirds to return in the spring, ready to take up their task as guardians of the bogs and of many parts of the shoreline as well. ◗

Greater yellowlegs are unique among Southeast sandpipers in that they feed extensively on small fish.

Drummers in the Woods

Woodpeckers! Six species of them are found in Southeast Alaska. They brighten gray days with the sound of their drumming and startle us with flashes of white, black, and red plumage.

·**Downy, hairy,** and **three-toed woodpeckers** live year-round in Southeast.

·**Northern flickers** and **red-breasted sapsuckers** generally leave the state in winter and return to nest in the spring.

· **Black-backed woodpeckers** occasionally occur in Southeast but are not known to nest here.

All woodpeckers depend on dead and rotting trees for nesting, and they contribute in important ways to the health of our forest and many of its other residents.

Northern Excavations, Inc.

Deep in a patch of woods somewhere in Southeast Alaska, a woodpecker clings tightly to the trunk of a big, aging hemlock tree. *Tap-tap-tap!* Again and again his strong, chisel-shaped beak sends wood chips flying 15 feet down to the forest floor as he painstakingly begins carving out what will become a hole for roosting or a nest cavity for his mate and their young.

The sound of his labors may echo through the forest for two or three weeks. By then, the persistent excavator will have completed a round, narrow entrance hole just large enough for him or his mate to slip through and a flask-shaped chamber inside the tree, maybe five, eight, or 10 inches wide and eight to 15 inches high.

A downy woodpecker, a rare year-round resident in Southeast Alaska. The red on the back of its head indicates it is a male.

Red-breasted sapsuckers are the most commonly seen woodpeckers in Southeast Alaska. The sugary sap that flows from the holes they excavate attracts hummingbirds, warblers, and kinglets as well as feeding the sapsuckers.

If the female woodpecker lays eggs inside the chamber, her young will be sheltered from the weather and well protected from predators during the few weeks they will need to mature before leaving the nest.

Great Adaptations

Chiseling into tree trunks is bone-wracking work, but our woodpecker has special physical characteristics that serve him well for both excavating cavities and ferreting out wood-boring insects and larvae to eat. His bill is heavy and strong, and its tip is flattened like a chisel. He has a thick skull and powerful neck muscles. Inside his skull he has a narrow space between the tough outer membrane of his brain and the brain itself. He is built to absorb the shock of pounding on wood day after day to make his living.

Other qualities contribute to his success as an excavator. He has short, strong legs and powerful thigh muscles. Strong feet with long toes and sharp claws help him grip the trunk of the tree. Stiff, pointed tail feathers help brace his body as his beak hammers away.

These same characteristics help downy, hairy, and three-toed woodpeckers feed by chiseling into tree trunks and the junctions and undersides of branches. They can pry into cracks and crevices or peel off bark to reach insects. One study during an epidemic infestation of Engelmann spruce beetles in Colorado found these three species of woodpeckers stripped the bark from heavily infested trees and fed on the overwintering brood of beetles. Beetle reduction by woodpeckers, the study reported, ranged

"The better to eat, my dear..."

Woodpeckers' tongues are specially adapted to their feeding habits. The tongues of downy, hairy, and three-toed woodpeckers have sharp, horny tips for spearing insects, while the tongues of flickers have small barbs useful for snatching insects from the ground. All four species have sticky saliva that helps make insects adhere to their tongues, and special organs called "Herbst's corpuscles" on the tips of their tongues, so they can feel prey they cannot see.

Sapsuckers have shorter tongues with brush-like tips for licking sap from the holes they drill in trees.

from 45 percent on lightly infested trees to 98 percent on heavily infested trees.

Red-breasted sapsuckers, the woodpeckers we see most often in Southeast, use their special woodpecker capabilities in a different way. They chisel rows of small rectangular holes into the bark of trees such as red alders and cottonwoods, then feed on sap and the soft cambium layer just beneath the bark. Over time, as sap oozes out of the holes, the woodpeckers return to feed. But some of their neighbors may share the banquet. The sugary sap may attract hummingbirds, other woodpeckers, kinglets, and even red squirrels and flying squirrels.

Northern flickers are the largest woodpeckers in Southeast, but they spend most of their time foraging on the ground. They can pluck insects from tree trunks and branches, but they eat berries as well. Like other woodpeckers, they use their strong bills to excavate nest holes.

The Hole Story

Alaska Department of Fish and Game biologist Jeff Hughes studied the types of trees in which woodpeckers excavate their nests in the Tongass National Forest. In an article published in the August 1988 issue of *Natural History* magazine, Hughes wrote:

> *Excavating birds almost always choose large, well-decayed western hemlocks that still retain most of their bark. (The bark keeps the interior wood moist, hastening heartrot, which softens the interior.) More than three-fourths of cavities are found in the upper third of hemlocks with missing or broken tops.*

"Good" woodpecker trees often have more than one cavity in them.

Woodpeckers may use the same cavities for nesting or roosting several years in a row, but often they do not. Instead their holes provide some of the best nesting sites for an amazing variety of other birds that are unable to excavate cavities themselves.

Among the birds that use woodpecker cavities in Southeast are Barrow's goldeneyes, buffleheads, American kestrels, western screech owls, northern pygmy owls, northern saw-whet owls, violet-green swallows, and tree swallows.

Chestnut-backed chickadees and red-breasted nuthatches use woodpecker holes, too, but they are also able to excavate nests themselves. Red squirrels and flying squirrels also may use woodpecker holes for denning, and in winter small birds that do not migrate south often shelter in them for the night.

Hughes's study led him to conclude that large, old trees are crucial to many birds in Southeast and that forest management should take this into account. He wrote:

> *Stands less than 100 years old rarely contain trees with heartwood decay. Without the well-decayed snags, at least twelve cavity-dependent bird species would not be able to find suitable nest sites in Tongass*

Northern flickers are most often seen in open forests. They feed often on the ground and sometimes along roadsides.

in summer, and nearly half of the forest's permanent avian residents would not find an adequate winter habitat. The result would be a much diminished forest.

Two woodpeckers—red-breasted sapsuckers and hairy woodpeckers—are among the animals considered "indicator species" in Southeast's coastal rain forest. This places them among brown bears, Sitka black-tailed deer, gray wolves, martens, and bald eagles as species whose population levels can be used to monitor the overall health of the forest and the way it is managed.

Private landowners can recognize the importance of woodpeckers, too, by leaving snags or trees with heartrot standing, or by knocking down only the top parts of dead trees and leaving lower sections to attract the excavations and rhythmic tappings of some of Southeast's most intriguing birds. ●

Not in My Backyard!

Bob's Recollections

Most of us hear woodpeckers before we see them. Perhaps we hear their loud, rhythmic drumming as they strike their bills against a hollow branch on a tree to proclaim their territory or to attract or bond with a mate. On occasion we might even be rudely awakened at dawn as an overzealous woodpecker uses our drainpipe, stovepipe, or metal trash can as a sounding board.

For woodpeckers, drumming serves the same purpose song does for many other birds. It proclaims a bird's territorial boundaries to others of its species.

My friend Dick Wood and I once instigated a demonstration of woodpecker territoriality. We carved a model of a black-backed woodpecker with legs made of nails and attached it to the trunk of a tree at eye level. Then we played a recording of a black-backed woodpecker drumming underneath it.

Within a few minutes a black-backed woodpecker flew to the model and attacked it, pecking fiercely at its head. As I took photos, the "real" woodpecker eventually knocked the "intruder" to the ground, then flew off and fed quietly nearby.

Apparently, bygones are bygones so long as one's territory remains intact.

Southeast's
Aquatic
Songbird

One winter's day in Southeast Alaska, as you walk or cross-country ski along some clear, burbling stream, you may be startled to hear a bird singing. A bird singing in winter? The song is beautiful—a series of high-pitched, melodic chirps and trills that seem to go on for a long time.

Soon you spot the source of the sound: a slate gray bird slightly smaller than robin, but with a short, stubby tail. It is perched in midstream on a rock that's half encircled by ice, and it is bobbing up and down like a small, wind-up toy.

When you approach, there is a whir of feathers, and the bird catapults into the air. Skimming just above the surface of the water, it flies directly over the path of the stream, veering left and right like a skier following a slalom course. Then it is gone.

You've just enjoyed one of Southeast's rare winter treats—the sight and sound of an American dipper. These plucky little birds—once called "water ouzels"—are Southeast's only aquatic songbirds.

Dippers can plunge into a raging stream, dive to the bottom, and emerge with food as if they were pulling lunch out of a washing machine agitating at full tilt. They swim underwater by flapping their partway-opened wings and kicking their legs. With their sharp beaks they poke and pry among rocks, ferreting out aquatic insects, or snatching small fish or eggs.

Dippers are the only Southeast "passerines"—perching birds or songbirds—specially adapted to survive in an underwater

In cold weather dippers fluff out their feathers to increase insulation. Dippers also have a thick layer of down beneath their outer feathers to maintain body heat.

(Above) Dippers can see as well underwater as in air. They feed on aquatic insects, fish, and fish eggs.

(Below) We've seen dippers swimming beneath the ice on frozen streams, but we wonder—When a dipper dives under the ice, how does it know there will be a way out at the other end?

environment. They have nasal flaps that keep water from entering their nostrils during dives. They have elongated toes with sharp claws for gripping rocks. They have a clear lens in the "nictitating" membrane that covers their eyes, so they can see as well underwater as in the air.

Dippers have more feathers covering their heads, necks, and bodies than songbirds of similar size, so they conserve body heat when they're immersed in cold water. They waterproof this "outer garment" by spreading oil on it from the uropygial gland above their tail.

Other birds do this as well, but in dippers the oil gland is 10 times larger than in songbirds of similar size, so they must do a lot of waterproofing! They also have a thick layer of down beneath their outer feathers, an excellent source of insulation like that found in ducks and other waterfowl.

Modified circulation also helps dippers function well underwater. To conserve oxygen during dives, they can decrease the blood supply to non-vital tissues and organs; and they have extra red blood cells so they can store more oxygen in their blood than most non-diving birds.

Some people believe they have seen dippers walking upstream along the bottoms of fast-flowing streams grasping rocks with their toes, but the birds probably do that only in shallow water. With their tight, waterproof plumage, dippers are actually very buoyant. When they're submerged they must "swim" with their wings continuously or they'll bob to the surface.

Dippers can also feed outside the water. Sometimes they leap above the surface to capture insects in flycatcher fashion, or fly low above the water, skimming insects from the surface or the air above.

Hidden nests

Perhaps as exciting as seeing a dipper would be finding a dipper nest, but that's far from easy. You'd be looking for a globe or dome about the size of a volleyball, made of moss and close to a fast-moving stream.

For protection from predators a nest would likely be hidden and inaccessible. It might be located under overhanging rocks or roots, behind a waterfall where the birds have to fly through the water to get to it, or perhaps under a bridge. The nests are almost completely enclosed, with only a small opening through which the parent birds can enter and exit.

Juneau ecologist Mary Willson found that dippers in the Juneau area were success-

ful in raising young more than 80 percent of the time. That rate is high compared to the 30 to 50 percent success typical of most small birds. Some dippers even raised two broods in a summer.

The importance of salmon

Former U.S. Forest Service biologist Kim Obermeyer and Willson studied dippers in 1998 and '99. They tracked nesting dippers on 10 streams around Juneau to see if the availability of salmon eggs and juvenile fish affected the birds' reproductive success.

The biologists banded more than 100 dipper nestlings and weighed them, sometimes several times throughout a season, to compare individual growth rates. They recorded what kinds of prey adult dippers brought to the nests, and how often they delivered it.

They also compared the nutritional value of the three types of prey most important to dippers: aquatic insects such as caddisfly larvae and stoneflies, chum and pink salmon eggs, and coho salmon fry.

They found that salmon fry had a higher content of protein, calcium, and phosphorus than aquatic insects. Salmon eggs, too, were more nutritious. One coho fry, for example, supplies three times as many calories as a single large aquatic insect, and one chum salmon egg has eight times the calories of one large aquatic insect.

On three of the streams studied, between 50 and 80 percent of the food adult dippers brought their nestlings was coho salmon fry.

During a less enlightened time, these findings might have branded dippers as a threat to salmon populations, as bald eagles and Dolly Varden were once thought to be. But dippers probably feed mostly on unburied eggs that won't survive; and most streams produce more coho fry than the streams can support. Dippers also feed on

sculpins, one of the major predators on salmon eggs. So it's unlikely that dippers have a detrimental effect on healthy salmon populations.

Why do dippers "dip"?

The behavior for which dippers are named is still a biological mystery. No one has been able to explain why the birds make their unusual dipping motion, bend-

When dippers feed their chicks salmon fry the chicks have a better survival rate.

Dipper nests are often wet on their outer surface. If the moss they are made of continues growing, the dippers raise their young in a "living" shelter. Inside, the nests are lined with soft grass and leaves that keep the nestlings dry.

ing their legs so their entire body moves up and down.

Some birding experts have suggested the movement up and down changes the light angle so the birds can see into the water, or that it's a means of communicating amid the noise of flowing water.

Dippers tend to dip more rapidly while courting, during territorial disputes, or when they are alarmed; and young birds practice dipping even while they're still in the nest. But dippers dip even when they are alone, so perhaps it's a kind of fitness exercise, warming up the muscles before the icy dive for a meal.

Whatever the reason, dippers are considered good indicators of water quality in streams. They can live and feed only where there is clear, running water, unpolluted and capable of sustaining substantial numbers of aquatic insects and young fish. That's one more reminder of the importance of protecting our fisheries and the waters and forests that nurture them.

Unlike most other songbirds, dippers sing their beautiful, melodious song year-round. Bill closed and throat inflated, this dipper is singing loudly.

Bob's Recollections

One summer I gained the confidence of a dipper family near Suicide Falls along Thane Road near Juneau. For four days, for three to four hours a day, I sat on a rock in the middle of a rushing stream. Eventually, the youngsters would crawl around over my feet, and the adults fed them right in front of me. It was a wonderful experience. The youngsters were

totally capable of eating on their own, but as soon as an adult came, they would jump up on a rock and beg to be fed.

These two photos were taken at that time.

THE SHOREbIRds ARE COMING!

By early April the days in Southeast Alaska are getting longer. In the woods and around homes, early blueberries are blooming; and in marshes and seeps, skunk cabbage is pushing up gleaming yellow spears. Woods and meadows are coming alive with the first bird songs, and there is one other much-awaited delight for Southeast residents and visitors—millions of shorebirds will soon descend upon our muddy shores and wetlands.

We see them in huge numbers between mid-April and the end of May—Greater yellowlegs dart this way and that, sweeping their bills from side to side as they search for small fish in the shallow intertidal sloughs.

Dowitchers jab at the mud, their bizarre-looking long bills probing like sewing machine needles. Turnstones walk slowly among rocks and globs of seaweed, turning them over with their bills and grabbing the creatures living under them before they can scurry away.

There'll be groups of small sandpipers, sometimes moving as one along the water's edge. They probe rapidly after small invertebrates, or dart after insects momentarily caught by the advancing tide. Suddenly, as a bald eagle flies over, they all take flight. Large and small, perhaps eight different species, they fly in unison. Whirling, shifting, flashing, they show first the different

Long-billed dowitchers are one of the most easily observed shorebirds during spring and fall migrations through Southeast Alaska.

61

*(Top) Rock sandpipers
in flight
(Middle left) Dunlins
(Bottom left) Common snipe
on its nest
(Above right) Semipalmated
plover at its nest*

wing and rump patterns of each species, then their white bellies—a choreographed blur too fast for our eyes to follow. Then, just as suddenly, they all land together and resume feeding.

Most of these shorebirds will be passing through Southeast as migrants. Leaving wintering areas often thousands of miles south of us, they are heading to Interior and Northern Alaska. There they will find large areas of wetlands, and long days of intense sunlight that make the wetlands incredibly rich in algae, aquatic plants, tiny crustaceans, mollusks, and insects.

Some shorebirds, like semipalmated plovers, killdeer, spotted sandpipers, and common snipes, come to Southeast to nest. And some, like dunlins, black turnstones, surfbirds, and rock sandpipers, are heading northward to nest after wintering in Southeast.

Flying Long and High

Shorebird migrations are one of the great wonders of the natural world, for shorebirds generally migrate even greater distances than most birds do. Bar-tailed godwits, occasionally seen in spring on the Mendenhall Wetlands in Juneau, may have traveled 6,800 miles from New Zealand; American golden-plovers come from southern South America; and red knots may come from as far away as Tierra del Fuego.

Shorebirds often make such trips in a few weeks or less, for they typically migrate both day and night. In many cases, they double their weight before leaving their wintering grounds, laying on fat to help fuel the long journey; then they set out against unknown weather and perilous dangers, across mountains, deserts, and hundreds or even thousands of miles of ocean.

Many shorebirds travel at high altitudes. Sandpipers have been found at 13,000 feet, over the Rocky Mountains. Bar-tailed godwits have been spotted at almost 20,000 feet.

And western sandpipers have been spotted on radar flying at 19,530 feet.

Some shorebirds can fly thousands of miles and for several days without stops, food, or water. But most depend upon stopping at crucial refueling points along the way. In recognition of the many crucial links in the chain of shorebird survival, a number of government agencies and organizations, including the Western Hemisphere Shorebird Reserve Network, are working to identify some of the places in North and South America that are crucial stopovers for migrating shorebirds.

Refueling Areas

Some 38 species of shorebirds are known to visit Southeast Alaska. The Alaska Shorebird Conservation Plan recognizes three sites that serve large numbers of the marathon travelers: the Stikine River Delta, Mendenhall Wetlands, and the Yakutat Forelands.

The U.S. Forest Service estimates that at least 22 shorebird species stop to refuel in the Stikine River Delta each year in April and May. With some 42 square miles of freshwater and tidal wetlands, the delta provides gravel, sand, mud beaches, sloughs, ponds, and tidal meadows where birds can rest and refuel, sometimes in flocks that include as

Spotted sandpipers are one of the few species of shorebirds that commonly nest in Southeast Alaska.

(Above left) A greater yellowlegs finishes grooming after bathing.

(Above right) A lesser yellowlegs takes a nap between bouts of feeding.

many as 100,000 birds. Only 10 miles north of Wrangell, the area draws birders and other visitors to view shorebirds as well as other wildlife. Since shorebirds seldom stop more than a few days at a time, the thousands of birds seen on different days or weeks are probably not the same individuals, but include newcomers taking the place of other birds that have traveled on.

At Mendenhall Wetlands, adjacent to the Juneau Airport and including the mouth of the Mendenhall River, birding enthusiasts have kept records of shorebird sightings for the past 16 years. They have counted hundreds and sometimes thousands of shorebirds, often in a single day, during April and May.

The species seen in greatest numbers have been ruddy turnstones, surfbirds, least sandpipers, pectoral sandpipers, dunlins, and short-billed dowitchers, but the most numerous of all are western sandpipers, which migrate through Southeast on their way from Central and South America to their breeding grounds in western Alaska.

Tracking a Speedy Migrant

Teams of researchers have been tracking western sandpipers along the West Coast from California to the Yukon Delta, so we know quite a bit about these remarkable little birds. Not much larger than most sparrows, western sandpipers winter in Central America and travel thousands of miles each spring to nest and raise their young in western or arctic Alaska. When researchers attached tiny radiotransmitters to 100 of these birds partway along the route in California and Washington, they discovered that the average sandpiper took 12 days to get from there to the Copper River Delta, where 65 percent of them were eventually picked up. But, the researchers reported:

> One 'phenomenal' female made the 3,200-kilometre [1,988-mile] trip from San Francisco Bay to Alaska's Copper River in less than 42 hours. To accomplish the feat she would have had to be traveling 80 kilometres [50 miles] an hour, non-stop. But the bird probably did stop, which means it was flying at up to 90 to 100 kilometres [56 to 62 miles] an hour.

In 1995 and '96, researchers found a number of sandpipers that had been radiotagged for the project on the Stikine Delta. They also learned that migrating sandpipers stopped for between one and three days at resting and refueling sites on their route north.

Here's how a Canadian biologist described what the sandpipers find on mudflats, such as those in key stopover areas like the Stikine:

Microscopic, single-celled algae that live in the mud migrate in between sediment grains and lay down mucous trails similar to trails produced by snails, which act to bind sediment grains together. The smooth surface of the mucous allows the incoming tidal waters to slip over the sediment instead of eroding it, creating a stable environment for invertebrates to live in. This microalgae also forms a primary food source for the mudflat food chain. Invertebrates such as worms and amphipods feed on this biofilm material and in turn are fed on by shorebirds, such as sandpipers.

Closer study revealed up to nine tiny worms per cubic centimeter in the mud, or "about 300 worms per average chocolate brownie slice," according to one researcher. It appears these worms are an important food for shorebirds, and sufficient densities of them may be crucial during the six-week period when tired and hungry shorebirds stop in the area on their way north.

Protecting Shorebirds

A growing understanding of how much shorebirds rely on critical areas in various countries, states, and regions has led to an international initiative to learn more about shorebirds and to protect the widely dispersed areas known to be important for their breeding, wintering, and rest and feeding during migration. Alaska is one of 12 regions in the United States that are developing conservation plans for shorebirds.

The Alaska Shorebird Working Group was formed in 1997 "to raise the visibility of shorebirds in Alaska, achieve consensus on needed conservation actions, and exchange information on issues, research findings, and education." In March 2002 the group released a "Conservation Plan for Alaska Shorebirds" that includes information gathered from research, objectives for protecting sustainable shorebird populations, and a review of issues affecting shorebirds.

More than 140 public and private organizations in seven countries are also cooperating to support the Western Hemisphere Shorebird Reserve Network, which compiles data, calls attention to places critical to shorebirds, and provides educational materials for teachers, students, and the general public.

Alaska's role in these hemisphere-wide efforts is an important one. We now know that 100 percent—*all*—of the North American populations of at least seven shorebird

(Above left) Amphipods are one of the most important foods for shorebirds during migration.

(Above right) Western sandpipers are the most numerous shorebirds seen in Southeast Alaska during migration.

species come to Alaska as either migrants or breeders. That includes an estimated 2.8 to 4.3 million western sandpipers—the most numerous of the spring visitors we see on the Stikine Delta and the Mendenhall Wetlands.

As a way station on the long, difficult path of migration, and as the breeding or wintering grounds for a few hardy species, Southeast Alaska plays an important part in keeping these populations healthy—for the enjoyment of residents and visitors alike, and because spring would not be spring without the abundant and uplifting presence of these most welcome harbingers of the season. ◗

What Shorebirds Eat

Aaron Baldwin (left) and Mary Willson conduct a timed sample for invertebrate species and abundance on the Mendenhall Wetlands in Juneau.

In 2003 Juneau ecologist Mary Willson and Aaron Baldwin, a graduate student at the University of Alaska Southeast, worked on the Mendenhall Wetlands to record the abundance and distribution of invertebrates such as amphipods, worms, and small clams—major foods on which migrating shorebirds depend.

They found that invertebrates were very numerous in areas of high bird use. In beds of mussels and fucus, and in areas of mixed sand and mud, they found polychaete worms, isopods, periwinkles, small clams, and amphipods (small, shrimp-like invertebrates).

In one area of mud flat Willson and Baldwin found a density of *Corophium* (a tiny amphipod) that translates to roughly 20,000 amphipods per square meter.

That's important because one study in the Bay of Fundy found that some sandpipers feed almost exclusively on *Corophium*. Each sandpiper consumed an estimated 30,000 of these amphipods per day.

Frequent Fliers

visit Southeast

From wintering grounds where they've waited out the lean and cold months, birds come to Alaska each spring in search of high energy food to get them through the season of nesting and rearing young.

Our still-extensive forests and their understory plants produce seeds and berries. Insects emerge from winter hiding. Wetlands spawn swarming clouds of mosquitoes, gnats, and midges. Young fish cluster in shallow water nurseries. And cold ocean waters burst with upwellings of nutrients, jump starting a food chain that will eventu-

ally feed untold numbers of seabirds, sea mammals, and humans.

By late spring Southeast's resident birds—chickadees, ravens, hairy woodpeckers, Vancouver Canada geese, and others—are joined by hordes of other avian adventurers.

Some will stay here all summer long. Others stop just long enough to rest and refuel, then continue to nesting grounds farther north.

Where do all the seasonal visitors come from? Decades of research are beginning to tell us.

Most of the sandhill cranes that come through Southeast Alaska wintered in California's Central Valley and Carrizo Plain.

67

(Above left) The Pacific-slope flycatcher nests throughout Southeast's coastal rainforest and migrates to the Neotropics for the winter.

(Above right) The subspecies of ruby-crowned kinglet that we see in Southeast winters from southwestern British Columbia to west central California.

(Opposite page) Rock sandpipers commonly nest in Western Alaska, but many spend the winter in Southeast.

Neotropical Migrants

Some 86 species, one-fourth of the bird species we might see in Southeast, are Neotropical migrants; that is, they breed in or migrate through Southeast Alaska then head for Mexico, Central America, or South America to spend the winter. A Pacific-slope flycatcher hawking insects from a Sitka spruce in June may have traveled 3,400 miles since leaving its winter home on the west coast of Mexico. A six-inch-long barn swallow nesting beneath the eaves of your garage may have flown 4,800 miles from Panama. And a greater yellowlegs plucking small fish from a tidal slough in Petersburg may have flown more than 9,000 miles from Tierra del Fuego at the southern tip of South America.

Vireos, most species of warblers, and shorebirds such as American golden-plovers also come to Southeast from places south of our nation's southern border.

Nearly all Neotropical migrants eat invertebrates. In summer they thrive on adult insects, insect larvae, and other foods in our forests, meadows, and wetlands. During the long daylight hours, perhaps with more space and fewer predators than in their winter homes, they are able to feed and raise young more successfully than they could if they stayed to the south.

Birds from British Columbia and the Lower 48

About a third of the bird species we see in Southeast each year have wintered in British Columbia and the Lower 48 states. Most of our trumpeter swans and northern pintail ducks migrate only as far as farmers' fields, productive marshes, and national wildlife refuges to the south. Trumpeter swans forage primarily in the fields of southwest British Columbia and western Washington. Alaska's northern pintails have strong ties to California, where about 85 percent of the pintails that breed in Alaska are estimated to overwinter.

Many of our land birds, such as varied thrushes and fox sparrows, also need migrate only to British Columbia and along the west coast to find sufficient berries and seeds to sustain them through the winter.

Birds from the North

About 12 percent of the bird species we see in Southeast during winter come from areas north of our region. They migrate to Southeast in fall after nesting and spend the winter with us. We have seen flocks of more than 500 long-tailed ducks feeding on tiny crustaceans near Douglas Island in midwinter, but come spring these birds head north. They may nest in Denali National Park or on the arctic coast of Alaska. Yellow-billed loons, looking like common loons except for their large, yellowish, upturned bills, are also here in winter, but come spring they head north. Some will perhaps nest on tundra lakes on the Seward Peninsula.

Rock sandpipers, which spend winters with us, commonly nest in the Aleutian Islands and on islands of the Bering Sea. A few owls that live up north year round sometimes visit Southeast in small numbers for the winter. For example, people in Haines have seen a northern hawk owl every winter for the past several years; and in winter of 2000 a great gray owl thrilled Juneau birders with a visit.

Where the Birds Come From

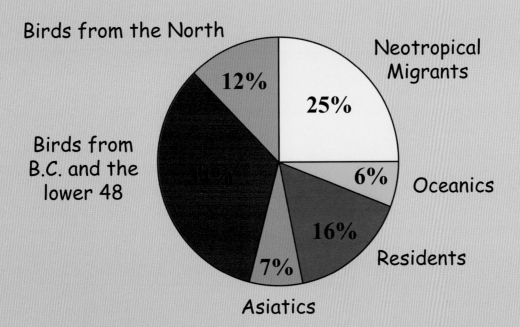

Birds from the North — 12%

Neotropical Migrants — 25%

Oceanics — 6%

Residents — 16%

Asiatics — 7%

Birds from B.C. and the lower 48

Some 336 species of birds have been seen in Southeast Alaska. This graph groups those species according to where we think most of their members come from.

(Above left) Red-necked phalaropes spend the winters in the open ocean of the South Pacific.

(Above right) Bramblings are Asiatic birds that occasionally wander into Southeast Alaska.

Oceanics

About six percent of the birds in Southeast come from or across the open ocean, often from islands and distant continents. Short-tailed shearwaters, gull-sized seabirds with long, slender wings, breed in southern Australia. An estimated 30 million of them migrate to the North Pacific in summer to feed. Red-necked phalaropes, which you can sometimes see spinning on the water to stir up food, winter on the open ocean in the South Pacific.

Long-tailed jaegers are agile sea birds that catch food in mid-air after they've chased gulls or terns and forced them to disgorge it. They come to Southeast after wintering off the coast of South America from Ecuador to Chile.

Parasitic jaegers follow migrating arctic terns to pirate food from them on their long journeys, then some of them settle down to nest on the Yakutat forelands.

Asiatics

Only about six percent of the birds that have been seen in Southeast come from Asia, but these are the species that serious birdwatchers may find most exciting.

The occurrence of these "Asiatics" in Alaska is facilitated by the state's closeness to Siberia. Though many of these species occur regularly in western Alaska, most of the ones we see in Southeast are vagrants. They have probably come quite by accident—perhaps because they were lost or blown off course by a storm.

That does not mean they are always reluctant to stay. A Steller's sea-eagle maintained residence up the Taku River near Juneau for several years, and a lesser black-backed gull once took up housekeeping in a colony of herring and glaucous-winged gulls at the face of Mendenhall Glacier.

Whenever Asiatics show up in Southeast, people try to see them, some even coming from distant parts of the United States and hiring helicopters or float planes to arrange a sighting, as in the case of the Steller's sea-eagle.

Eurasian wigeons are usually seen every year in the spring among American wigeons passing through Southeast or stopping here to breed. A European golden-plover was discovered one winter by a birder in Ketchikan. And sharp-tailed sandpipers, which closely resemble our common migrants, pectoral sandpipers, are seen in Southeast Alaska almost every year during fall.

Residents

About 53 species, or 16 percent of the bird species found in Southeast, live here year round. Blue grouse, adult bald eagles, American dippers, and other "resident" birds stay because they can find enough to eat throughout the year.

Blue grouse, which eat insects, buds, and flowers most of the year, have special bacteria in their gut that help them digest spruce needles, one of the few foods they can find in the winter. The bald eagles you see flapping across winter landscapes survive winter by finding fish and snatching occasional ducks and gulls. American dippers eat primarily aquatic insects, which are abundant in our streams all year round. Common ravens seem to take advantage of anything edible, including winter-killed deer, road-killed porcupines, and garbage from dumpsters and garbage cans.

Staying in Southeast year-round has several advantages. Resident birds face none of the perils of long journeys. They can begin nesting before migrant birds arrive, often laying a larger number of eggs and sometimes having time to raise more than one brood per season. But in return they must survive the rigors of winter, with less food, shorter daylight in which to feed, and temperatures that require extra energy in order to keep warm.

Worldwide Connections

The fact that 84 percent of the species seen here come from elsewhere does say something important to those of us living in Southeast. It reminds us that what happens here depends very much on what happens in other parts of the world where those birds spend their time.

It also reminds us we are a crucial link in the yearly cycle each of those species goes through in order to survive. For birds facing the rigors and perils of long-distance travel, every part of the itinerary—breeding grounds, wintering grounds, and stopover points where they rest and fuel up are all crucial to their survival. As with any chain, the migration patterns are only as strong as their weakest link.●

(Above left) This female blue grouse is a good example of a bird that stays in Southeast Alaska year-round.

(Above right) Some barn swallows fly nearly 5,000 miles from the Neotropics to nest in Southeast Alaska.

Wetland Stopovers in Southeast Alaska

(Top photo) More than 10,000 snow geese visit the Stikine River Delta every year.

(Above) This male snow goose seen on the Mendenhall Wetlands May 3, 2002, had been banded July 14, 2001, and had hatched in summer 2000, on Russia's Wrangel Island in the Chukchi Sea.

Migratory birds cannot survive without places to stop, rest, and refuel during their long journeys. For shorebirds these places are especially important because of the long distances that most species fly. The Conservation Plan for Alaska Shorebirds lists three such places in Southeast Alaska that are important for birds needing to rest and refuel during their long journeys. These places have value for other birds as well. In general what's good for a sandpiper is also good for ducks, geese, and even such songbirds as Lapland longspurs and horned larks and the migrating owls, falcons, and hawks that feed on them.

· **The Stikine River Delta near Wrangell** is the largest coastal marsh in Southeast Alaska. It is an important refueling area for sandhill cranes, more than 10,000 snow geese, and many other waterfowl as well as hundreds of thousands of shorebirds. Shorebird numbers usually peak around the first week in May. Almost 2,000 eagles are attracted to the delta's spring run of eulachon—the largest reported springtime concentration of bald eagles in North America.

· **The Mendenhall Wetlands** is the premier spot in Juneau for birds and birders. A total of 218 different species of birds have been seen in this area. That includes 40 species of shorebirds and 34 species of waterfowl. Shorebird and waterfowl numbers often reach into the thousands during the last week in April and during May.

· **The Yakutat Forelands** hosts over 100,000 shorebirds each year during migration. The spring bird migration begins in April. Thousands of gulls, geese, and sea ducks can be observed, as can hundreds of swans and sandhill cranes. The main wave of bird migrations passes through the last week of April and the first week of May. The fall bird migration begins in September, bringing sandhill cranes, Canada geese, snow geese, tundra swans, and waterfowl. More than 2,000 Aleutian terns nest within the forelands making this the largest known Aleutian tern colony in the world.

One other migratory stopover in Southeast Alaska should also be mentioned:

· **The Dude Creek Critical Habitat Area** near Gustavus includes a large expanse of undisturbed wet meadow. Most notably it feeds and shelters flocks of sandhill cranes migrating to and from their nesting areas around the Alaska Peninsula, Bristol Bay, Kenai Peninsula, and upper Cook Inlet. These birds also stop on the Stikine River Delta enroute to their wintering grounds in the Central Valley of California.

An arctic tern may have traveled more than 9,000 miles from Antarctica to nest on the Mendenhall Wetlands in Juneau.

Facts about Migratory Birds

Some Basic Facts

• Migration is triggered by changing length of daylight.

• Birds migrate for food, not because of weather.

• Most songbirds migrate at night, when the air is more stable and temperatures are cool.

• Hawks migrate in the daylight, soaring on winds and thermals.

• Shorebirds and waterfowl migrate both day and night when the weather is favorable.

Mechanisms for Navigation

• visual landmarks (raptors, waterfowl)

• the sun or solar compass (hawks, swifts, swallows)

• the stars or stellar compass (flycatchers, thrushes, warblers)

• the earth's magnetic fields (probably all birds)

• olfactory cues (storm-petrels)

A Gauntlet of Perils

• storms, especially when crossing open water

• loss of refueling habitat (over 50 % loss of wetlands in the Lower 48)

• loss of wintering habitat (especially loss of forests in the Neotropics)

• hitting communication towers, especially lighted ones (An estimated five million birds are killed in the U.S. each year in collisions with towers.)

• hitting windows (One study shows that each year more than 100 million migrating birds die crashing into windows.)

• predators (Studies show cats alone kill hundreds of millions of songbirds every year in the U.S.)

Songbirds in Winter

By December most song birds commonly found in Southeast Alaska have flown south. Yet a few species remain and, because they often visit our backyards, they are sometimes more easily seen in winter than in summer. How do they cope with wind, cold, snow and ice, limited hours of daylight, and shortages of food? Some eat different foods, or change their behavior to suit the season.

Common redpolls are known to burrow under the snow at night, where the temperature is several degrees warmer than at the surface.

Flocking up

Chestnut-backed chickadees gather in flocks before winter. This allows them to feed more efficiently and appears to serve some social purpose, such as helping to find and choose mates. Each flock establishes a territory that it defends from other flocks, sometimes dominating feeders and food sources within a 20-acre area. Within a flock, there is a definite pecking order. Some mated pairs are dominant over other pairs, and all pairs are dominant over single birds.

Chickadees, which feed mostly on seeds, insect larvae, and spiders, practice what is called *scatter hoarding*. Rather than eating food where they find it, they typically pick up one seed or insect at a time, fly off with it, and store it in one place—in a crack in the bark of a tree, beneath dead leaves, among lichens, in a knothole, and even within dirt or snow. Scattering food this way hides it from squirrels and otherbirds that could quickly make off with a single large stash.

Researchers found that black-capped chickadees, which are very closely related to

Southeast's chestnut-backs, can remember for up to 30 days where each seed has been stored. In fact, the hippocampus, the part of the brain associated with memory storage and spatial learning, is proportionately larger in chickadees than in birds that do not cache food. Researchers also found that in chickadees, that part of the brain grows considerably larger in October, just before the birds begin their winter scatter hoarding.

Within each chickadee flock dominant birds get the best places to store seeds, just as in spring dominant pairs get the best of the limited nesting areas available. There are also young, low-ranked birds called "floaters" that move as individuals from one flock to another. They rank below the regular flock members, but if one of the partners of the top two or three pairs in a flock dies, a floater will pair with the survivor, providing it is of the opposite sex. In this way, the floater becomes part of a dominant pair, gaining better access to food and to breeding territory in the spring.

Other winter birds such as kinglets, brown creepers, and nuthatches often travel with chickadee flocks. They probably do this partly to take advantage of the flock's collective knowledge about where to find food within a particular territory.

During cold weather, small birds like chickadees have to eat every day to survive. One study showed that a chickadee waking up on a winter morning could not survive the day and the following night without eating. At night members of the flock roost together, usually amid dense foliage or in tree cavities. Individuals may lower their body temperature as much as 8 to 12 degrees Centigrade to save energy. *(See "Chilling Out" later in this book.)*

In winter chickadees typically store food in times of plenty and retrieve it when food becomes scarce.

Going where the food is

Several other species of seed-eating birds also winter in Southeast Alaska. Red and white-winged crossbills, pine siskins, and common redpolls are finches—sparrow-like birds with short, conical beaks used to crack open seeds. All four of these are called *irruptive species* because they travel quite widely in relation to cone crops, which generally follow "boom and bust" cycles over the years. Each irruptive species specializes at extracting seeds from certain cones such as spruce, hemlock, birch, or alder. Wherever their associated tree cones are abundant, these species will be abundant. When cone production is poor, bird numbers decline drastically, as the birds move elsewhere. Red and white-winged crossbills, for example, move back and forth across boreal forests from Alaska to Newfoundland, visiting Southeast when cones and the seeds within them are plentiful.

Red and **white-winged crossbills,** which use their crisscross bills and long tongues to extract seeds from between the bracts of cones, are like small, acrobatic parrots. Though they are difficult to identify from a distance, they are often the birds you can barely see flitting about in the tops of coniferous trees. Occasionally they will

come to feeders, the males with bright red plumage, the females in feathered tones of olive and gray.

Unlike most of our other birds, which nest only in spring and early summer, crossbills may nest and raise young in winter. They build their nests in the dense foliage of spruce trees during January through April. Both parents feed their young regurgitated clumps of whole seed kernels that are covered with a viscous material.

To cope with Southeast's short winter days, crossbills may have to forage constantly for more than 90 percent of the daylight hours. Unlike chickadees, they do not cache food, but they do have a kind of side pocket in their esophagus that can store more than one gram of seeds to be processed later.

Small brownish-streaked **pine siskins** also travel in flocks around Southeast in winter. Siskins have a touch of yellow on their wings and at the base of their tail, the color intensifying as the birds mature. Although siskins often travel about in huge winter flocks, they don't seem to get along well with one another. They seem to fight and try to displace each other almost constantly, all the while uttering their scratchy *shick-shick* calls interspersed with occasional long, buzzy *schhreeees*.

Other songbirds that winter in Southeast Alaska:
(Top left) Pine siskin
(Top right) Common redpoll
(Lower left) Pine grosbeak
(Lower right) Bohemian waxwing

Steller's jays are year-round residents in Southeast and usually begin nesting in early spring.

We have seen adult siskins feeding begging juveniles in early April, when snow still covered the ground, so we suspect that, like crossbills, siskins sometimes nest during Southeast winters.

Common redpolls, other flocking seed-eaters, are small brownish-streaked birds with bright red caps, blackish chins, and a pinkish wash on their breasts. Like crossbills, redpolls have an outpocketing in their esophagus in which they can store seeds to be eaten later. This enables them to gather food quickly in places where they are exposed to cold weather and predators. Then they fly to sheltered places where they regurgitate, shell the seeds, and swallow them at their leisure. Because of this special adaptation, a redpoll can gather enough food toward the end of a short winter day to survive the long, cold night.

Redpolls are also known to burrow under the snow at night, where the temperature is usually several degrees warmer than at the surface.

In winter redpolls eat the seeds of grasses, sedges, and weeds, if the plants are not covered by snow. Winter flocks can also be seen knocking seeds from the catkins of willows and alders that extend above the snow, then gathering them up from the ground or snow below.

Some trees and shrubs in Southeast hold their berries well into winter and may be especially attractive to birds. In towns and cities where European mountain ash have been introduced, winter flocks of **Bohemian waxwings** and **pine grosbeaks** may sweep through neighborhoods, gorging themselves and stripping the trees of their bright red berries. These two species are often amazingly tame. We suspect they sometimes become a little inebriated from eating the slightly fermented berries!

Banking on spring

Perhaps the noisiest and most visible winter birds in Southeast are **Steller's jays,** which often dominate backyard bird feeders by their sheer size and boldness. Sometimes unwelcome at feeders, they seem to have all the cleverness and creativity of squirrels in devising ways to get more than their share of winter food.

Jays have a special throat pouch they can use to store food. They then can carry off extra food and cache it to be eaten later. This allows them to nest earlier in spring than most other Southeast birds: they can rely on cached food and sometimes cached nest materials to get a jump on the season.

Their sounds and calls make Steller's jays especially interesting. Only male jays give a high, muted whistle, usually on one pitch, while females make a mechanical-sounding rattle. In late winter or early spring the male courts the female with a "whisper song" that is surprisingly musical, a medley of whistled and gurgled notes interspersed with snapping or popping sounds run together. ●

Feeding Birds

Putting out food is a great way to lure birds close to your home so you can watch them in winter. It's good to put out a variety of foods if you want to attract a variety of birds.

Black oil sunflower seeds attract chickadees, jays, and pine siskins. Standard seed mixes are usually high in millet, which will attract sparrows and jays. Suet, which provides fat important to birds in very cold weather, will likely attract chickadees, woodpeckers, and nuthatches. Thistle is expensive but is a favorite of wintering pine siskins.

Some stores offer shelled sunflower seeds, which sell for more per pound than unshelled seeds, but in the long run they may be less expensive because they're all food, and they won't disappear as fast as seeds with shells. They also dispense with scrap piles of discarded shells around feeder areas.

Watching Birds

Once birds start coming to your feeder you will have the fun of watching their antics and trying to identify different species. This is a chance to learn about bird behavior, too. Consider such questions as:

• How do different kinds of birds approach the feeder? What foods do different species prefer?

• What differences do you see in birds' flight as they approach or leave? Where do they approach from and then fly to?

• How do different kinds of birds grasp food—with feet, beaks? Do they take one seed or several before flying away? Do they feed for long periods, or in brief, interrupted moments?

• How do birds protect themselves from predators while they're eating? Do some birds seem to serve as lookouts? Do species differ in how close you can approach them?

Rare Sightings

A high point of feeding birds is the possibility of attracting a rare bird. Rare birds sighted at Southeast Alaska feeders have included a spotted towhee, a white-throated sparrow, a mountain chickadee, and a black-throated blue warbler, none of which are normally found here.

Chestnut-backed chickadees can be extremely tame. With patience you can train them to eat sunflower seeds from your open palm.

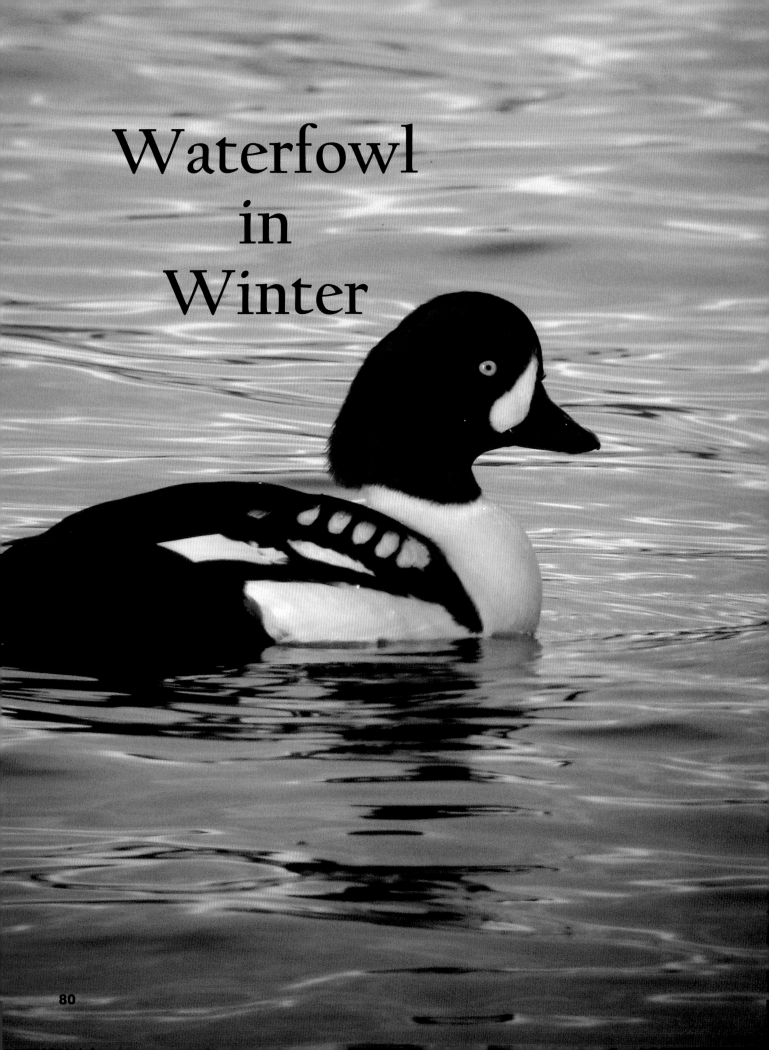

Waterfowl
in
Winter

During a cold winter in Southeast Alaska, a bitter wind whips along the beach. Rocks and gravel glisten with ice. Even in sheltered inlets the water is frosted with whitecaps, and its temperature has dropped to a seasonal average of about 42°F.

A few hundred feet offshore 30 or more sea ducks—warm-blooded animals that must maintain a certain body temperature to survive—bob on the waves. Every few moments, as if they were taking turns, individual ducks dive headfirst beneath the surface, popping up moments later like corks shot from some underwater popgun.

Southeast Alaska is a Mecca for sea ducks in winter. All eight species found in North America can be seen here then—buffleheads, harlequin ducks, long-tailed ducks, Barrow's and common goldeneyes, and black, white-winged, and surf scoters. How do these birds survive the cold, especially when they spend so much time submerged in cold water?

that help conserve body heat by trapping pockets of air. Covering that is an outer layer of contour feathers that pack closely together and have interlocking barbs, so the birds are virtually waterproofed—another characteristic that conserves heat.

Spreading oil that they take from a gland at the base of the tail may help birds waterproof the outer feathers, but this has not been proven. Spreading oil on the feathers while preening may be more important to protect the feathers against fungi, bacteria, and lice that would damage them.

Some sea ducks have down as much as two-thirds of an inch thick in places. It is usually thickest on their underside, the part of the body most exposed to water and thus likely to lose heat the fastest. Birds in northern areas like Southeast have more fat and feathers than birds of the same or similar species living father south, so they are better equipped to deal with cold temperatures. In extremely cold weather sea ducks also shake their feathers after a dive, throwing off drops of water that could otherwise quickly freeze.

What keeps the ducks in Southeast during cold weather is the ready supply of food.

Sea ducks have wonderful natural insulation—a kind of avian equivalent to the human population's Polarfleece® parkas and Gore-tex® rain jackets. They have a thick layer of fat just beneath the skin that helps keep them warm. Outside their skin is a thick layer of down—short, fluffy feathers

Harlequin ducks are year-round residents in Southeast and are the only sea ducks that commonly nest here.

Buffleheads are one of the most easily observed sea ducks. They generally feed in open fresh or salt water relatively close to shore.

(Preceding page) Barrow's goldeneye, male

Sea ducks eat small crabs, clams, shrimp, limpets, chitons, mussels, amphipods, barnacles, sea urchins, sea stars, marine worms, small fish, and algae—all foods that are available in winter as well as in summer.

Swans with gray plumage are juveniles, which overwinter with their parents.

Although most **trumpeter swans** nest to the north and winter to the south, a few trumpeters winter in Southeast, where they add an elegant snowy white presence to gray winter days. Peter Walsh, a dedicated birder in Petersburg, for many years reported that an average 100 swans a year wintered in Blind Slough near Petersburg. A small flock sometimes numbering up to 30 swans has also wintered over at Snettisham, south of Juneau, for at least the past 12 years.

Vancouver Canada geese are the only subspecies that breeds and winters in Southeast Alaska.

During very cold weather the swans sit down on land with their feet and legs tucked beneath their thickly feathered bellies, and their heads tucked back under their wings. This posture is one way birds can reduce heat loss from parts of their bodies that have the least insulation—their unfeathered legs

and feet, and their heads, especially around their eyes.

Swans' ability to feed at night is an advantage in winter because it allows them to be active and generating body heat during the coldest hours, while they can rest during daylight hours, when it is likely to be warmest.

Southeast Alaska's **Vancouver Canada geese** are year-round residents, not to be confused with smaller, paler subspecies that migrate through many wetland areas in the spring. According to Jim King, a wildlife biologist who lives near the Mendenhall Wetlands in Juneau, 500 to 600 Vancouver Canada geese spend the winter on the wetlands, and they seem to have adapted their habits to fit the human calendar. King says that although the birds vacate the wetlands during hunting season, by mid-October they often come in to feed at night when the hunters are elsewhere.

Soon after hunting ends in mid-December, the geese return to the wetlands, and they stay there day and night until early April, when the paired adults move to their nesting sites at such areas as Seymour Canal on Admiralty Island.

Geese, ducks, and swans all share a fascinating winter adaptation that helps them overcome the problem of heat loss and possible freezing in their bare, unfeathered legs and feet. Ducks swimming in 34-degree water, or geese standing on a frozen lake, could lose a great deal of heat through their extremities. But they don't.

The arteries and veins in their legs lie next to each other, and this minimizes heat loss. When chilled blood from the feet moves through the veins toward the body, it picks up heat from the adjacent arteries, which carry blood that is warmer because it is coming from the bird's body core. At the same time, as warmed blood from the bird's body core moves through the arteries toward the feet, it is cooled by the nearby veins, and

there is less warmth to be lost where the foot or leg is exposed to cold air, water, or ice. Under extremely cold conditions, the birds can further reduce heat loss by constricting the blood vessels in their feet and reducing the amount of blood flow.

Because of this natural heat exchange, a duck standing on a frozen lake may have a body core temperature of 104°F but a foot temperature only slightly above freezing. Considering that bare feet and legs lose heat about four times as fast when they are immersed in water as when they are exposed to air, the importance of this amazing feature is pretty clear, especially for swimming and wading birds.

Winter in Southeast Alaska is not an easy time, yet sea ducks, swans, and geese have adapted to weathering the winter in remarkable ways. We can only marvel at how they survive raging storms, ice, and cold while we sit cozy and warm in our heated homes. ●

Waterfowl like the female mallard above are specially adapted to avoid heat loss from their legs and feet.

Waterfowl Courting

Sea ducks that winter in Southeast waters may spend part of the season courting. From January to May watch for some of this fascinating behavior:

• Male goldeneyes court females by dipping their bills in the water, raising their heads straight up, and then bending their heads clear over onto their backs while uttering a peculiar whistle. Competition is often intense. In the photo above and to the right, five males are courting a single female.

• Male buffleheads perform a head-bobbing, chin-up display with their head feathers erected.

• Male long-tailed ducks spring excitedly into flight, dashing madly about, then abruptly splash back down into the water.

• Male harlequins make a mouselike squeaking sound or a low whistle that ends in a long trill.

Despite all this courtship activity, only harlequins, of all sea ducks, commonly nest in Southeast. Come spring, the mature adults of most sea ducks fly north, while subadults of some species, such as scoters, stay behind.

The
Perfect
Predators

Some animals—like the moose with its gangly legs and bulbous nose—seem as if they might have been designed by a committee. It's not immediately obvious how all their parts work together.

So it's all the more fascinating to see a family of animals such as the owls, whose every physical feature and capability seems honed for a single purpose: to hunt down and capture the small mammals (and sometimes birds) that are their most important food.

Six different species of owls are regularly seen or heard in Southeast Alaska, and four others visit our region occasionally. All these owls live by feeding on other animals—primarily mice, voles, and occasionally birds. To capture these prey, owls have some remarkably powerful senses, the most important of which are hearing and sight. In fact, ornithologist Paul A. Johnsgard wrote: "The heads of owls are basically little more than brains with raptorial beaks and the largest possible eyes and ears attached."

Ears to Hear With

Owls have better hearing than any other bird. Many owls can locate prey by sound alone—when it is in tall grass, beneath the snow, or somewhere around them in total darkness. They have very large eardrums for their size, and large vertical ear-openings bordered with flaps at the front side (and sometimes also the back). The ear openings are surrounded by the owls' trademark facial disks—ruffs of stiff, dark-tipped feathers that work as reflectors, channeling even very faint sounds to the ears.

Owls can control the movement of both their ear flaps and the surrounding feathers, and they use them much as you might cup a hand in *front* of your ear to concentrate sounds coming from behind you. When an owl detects a sound it turns its head toward it, sometimes swiveling its head more than 180 degrees to face directly behind itself.

Owls can pinpoint where sounds are coming from because their right and left ear openings differ in size and are not located symmetrically. Owls' heads are also very broad, so the openings are relatively far apart. As a result, two things happen: There is a slight difference in the time it takes for a sound to reach each ear, and there is a difference in the intensity of the sound that reaches each ear. Together these differences help owls zone in on sounds. They may hear a mouse rustling through the grass, or small birds twittering and jostling for space as they roost together on a tree branch for the night.

> **"The heads of owls are basically little more than brains with raptorial beaks and the largest possible eyes and ears attached."**

One study found, in fact, that a great gray owl can locate prey under as much as a foot and a half of snow (and in pursuit of such prey it can break through a snow crust strong enough to support a 176-pound man).

Great horned owls are one of the fiercest owls and have been known to attack prey many times their own weight.

(Preceding page) A boreal owl returns to its nest with a small bird it has caught.

The forward edges of the feathers on an owl's wings are serrated (unlike those of other birds, which are smooth). When owls are flying this irregularity disrupts the flow of air over their wings and eliminates the vortex noise created by air flow over a smooth surface. As a result, owls can fly more quietly than other birds. This gives them great stealth in pursuing their prey, but it may be equally important in allowing the owls to hear as they swoop or glide toward prey they can hear but not see.

Eyes to See With

Owls also have exceptionally good vision. Their eyes are large compared to those of many other animals. (A two-foot-long snowy owl, for example, has an eyeball almost as large as a six-foot-tall man's.) So owls see larger and sharper images than a person or many other species of birds would.

They also have large numbers of "rods" (the photosensitive receptors in the eye that allow animals to see in dim light), and their pupils open widely in the dark. According to some studies, the eyes of certain owls have nearly six times better light-gathering power than human eyes have.

Owls may be the only birds with true stereoscopic, or three-dimensional, vision. This means that their prey stands out from its background. It is easier to see, and the owl can pinpoint its position to make an accurate strike.

Owls also have telescopic vision. Their eyes are located within long, bony sockets, so the eyeballs are elongated. That gives them a long focal length, much like the telescopic lens on a camera. They can focus well on distant objects.

Owls do have a relatively narrow field of view, (about a third of what humans have), and their eyeballs do not move. But owls simply turn their heads to see around them, just as they do to locate sounds.

Strong Talons, Camouflage, and Patience

Owls have strong, sharp talons on all four of their toes, and they often swing their outer, or fourth, toes backward. That gives the talons a two-in-front, two-in-back arrangement so they have maximum spread and maximum strength for striking or carrying prey.

One study demonstrated the tremendous strength this gives to owls as predators. The study showed it took a force of more than twenty-eight and a half pounds to open the talons of a great horned owl.

Jim King, a wildlife biologist in Juneau, told us of an incident in which a great horned owl killed a healthy captive trumpeter swan that was unable to reach water to escape the owl's attack. The owl weighed 2.6 pounds. The swan weighed 26 pounds.

With strength owls combine stealth. Besides being able to fly silently, they are cryptically colored. Their mostly brown, gray, and black feathers blend in well with their surroundings (and the white plumage of snowy owls blends well with snow). Most owls hunt by remaining still, perched on branches and watching or listening for their prey.

But even the best predators must be prepared to deal with hard times. When food is abundant owls may cache their prey to be eaten later. If the prey become hard frozen in winter, the owls defrost it in a rather unusual manner: They sit on it and warm it as if they were incubating an egg.

Owls such as the short-eared and northern pygmy hunt mostly by day. Others such as the northern saw-whet, western screech, great horned, and barred hunt mostly by night.

From the perspective of a mouse or vole—or even a small bird—there is no time of day or night when you cannot be captured by an owl.

Owls *regularly* seen in Southeast Alaska include: great horned owl, northern pygmy owl, western screech-owl, northern saw-whet owl, barred owl, and short-eared owl. (See following pages) Owls *occasionally* seen in Southeast Alaska include: northern hawk owl, boreal owl, snowy owl, and great gray owl.

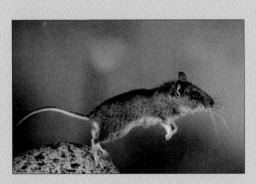

What's for Dinner?

Small mammals such as voles and mice are common prey of most owls in Southeast Alaska. We know this because after they have eaten, owls regurgitate the undigestible parts of their meal: bones, feathers, beaks, skulls, fur, and teeth.

These photos show (*top left*) a deer mouse, (*top right*) a red-backed vole, and (*bottom right*) a pellet dropped by a short-eared owl. The pellet is surrounded by skulls and jawbones of long-tailed voles that were extracted from other pellets found in the same area.

Owls Regularly Found in Southeast Alaska

With Bob's Recollections

Great Horned Owl
Southeast's most common breeding owl—a formidable predator
Length 18-25 inches

I started a lifetime fascination with owls at the age of 12. I grew up close to a state game farm where they routinely trapped and disposed of owls that preyed on the quail and pheasants. I wanted to rescue one nice-looking great horned owl and asked if I could have it to raise as a pet. With my fingers crossed behind my back, I told the workers I would never release it.

That's how I got "Hoot." He would perch on my shoulder or arm and accept food from my hand. My friends and I especially liked to take Hoot along as a watch-owl when we went camping. He would perch near our camp, and if someone or something approached, Hoot would rapidly snap his beak and hiss, so we knew someone was coming. I always wrapped a piece of leather around my forearm where Hoot perched, but even so I can remember the tremendous pressure of his grip.

I decided to release Hoot after a couple of months, which was probably a good thing. I later read of several people who were injured when they approached too close to a great horned owl's nest, and of one photographer who was blinded while attempting to photograph a nesting great horned owl.

Northern Pygmy Owl
A tiny sparrow-size owl whose plumage includes "false eyes" at the back of its neck
Length 7 inches

One spring when I was walking along the Dike Trail at the Juneau Airport, a northern pygmy owl flew out of a tree and snatched a small shrew almost at my feet. Ignoring me completely, it flew back to the tree and proceeded to eat the tiny brown creature while I watched at eye level from about two feet away.

Western Screech-Owl
A feisty, seldom seen nocturnal hunter
Length about 8-1/2 inches

One good way to determine if there are any owls in your area is to walk along at night and play a recording of the calls of different species—especially during breeding season in March and April. If an owl is within hearing distance it will usually answer.

A number of years ago several of us were told that a western screech-owl had been seen along Basin Road close to the old Perseverance Mine near Juneau. In hopes of hearing or seeing it, we walked along the road one night during the spring. I carried a tape recorder over my shoulder and occasionally played the call of a western screech-owl. I got an unexpected answer. Before I knew what was happening, a screech-owl fluttered against the tape recorder, then quickly flew away. I'm not sure whether it was defending its territory or thought I was a potential mate.

Northern Saw-whet Owl
A tame and retiring nocturnal hunter that feeds mostly on deer mice
Length 7-1/2 inches

Some friends told me they saw a northern saw-whet owl one September when they were hunting deer at Gambier Bay. They were deep in the woods, and were startled to come upon the little owl perched on a horizontal branch only about eight feet above the ground. Unlike the Steller's jays that had been dashing about and scolding them throughout the afternoon, the owl sat without moving, even as the two hunters walked directly beneath its perch.

I have read of people being able to pick up and handle these seemingly very tame little owls during the daytime. Like other small owls, northern saw-whets nest in tree cavities. If disturbed at their nest, they usually refuse to leave the cavity.

Barred Owl
More often heard than seen. Call is a series of distinctive and emphatic hoots that rise in intensity and sound like hoo hoo hoo hoo hoo hoo hu-HOOOOOO!
Length 17-24 inches

One day in 1977 Frank Glass, a Juneau birder, sighted what would have been the first barred owl seen in Alaska. It was on a trail bordering Peterson Creek about a mile past the end of North Douglas Road near Juneau. To establish his sighting as an official record, Frank needed a photograph or a recording.

That evening at twilight I joined Frank in an effort to find the owl again and record its voice. We walked along the trail for about three hours periodically playing a recording of a barred owl, but we got no response.

Disappointed, we returned to the car and decided to play the recording one last time. The owl immediately answered us from a tree right next to the car. The recording was made and Frank's record was established.

Short-eared Owl
Southeast's most easily observed owl because it hunts during the day over open country
Length 15 inches

Jack Helle, a biologist with the National Marine Fisheries Service Auke Bay Laboratory near Juneau, once observed a short-eared owl snatching swimming voles from the water on the Mendenhall Wetlands in Juneau. On extreme high tides voles that live near the tideflats are often surprised by the advancing water and are forced to swim. This owl was apparently taking advantage of the voles' dilemma. At one point Jack saw the owl dive—feet first—completely under water and emerge with a vole in its talons.

Fish

Dolly Varden

Fish in Southeast Alaska

Quillback rockfish

A total of 521 fish species are known to occur in all of Alaska. Of these, 309 or 59 percent are in the waters of Southeast Alaska. Other than the relatively few species that are important for commercial, sport, or subsistence fisheries, little is known about most fish in the state.

Thanks to the book *Fishes of Alaska* published in 2002, we have a pretty good idea of what species occur here and their distribution and descriptions. What we lack is information on the behavior and natural history of the majority of these species. This is unfortunate because fish are really characters.

Bob worked as a fish biologist with the Alaska Department of Fish and Game for 23 years, and he also taught courses about fish at the University of Alaska in Fairbanks and in Juneau. He remembers, when he was studying the territorial behavior of young coho and Dolly Varden in the field, that each stream pool contained a despot—a fish that was dominant over all others in the pool. If a subordinate happened to grab food near or in the despot's territory, the despot would cruise the entire pool and attack all the fish it encountered. Those observations and many others that followed convinced him that fish are indeed individuals and can exhibit behavior—perhaps not so different from our own.

Once you think of fish as individuals (perhaps even characters) they then become not so different from the birds and mammals we tend to spend more time watching.

Because of Bob's background we could have included many more articles on fish, but we did not know of many studies that provide interesting and engaging information about them. We did, however, find a few.

To help celebrate a few really strange fish characters we wrote the article on "Weird Fish." It helped a lot that Bob was allowed to photograph these fish in the wonderful aquariums maintained at DIPAC hatchery and the National Marine Fisheries Service Auke Bay Laboratory, both in Juneau.

The article on "The Gifts of Salmon" was prompted by the work of three ecologists at the Forestry Sciences Laboratory in Juneau. Mary Willson, Scott Gende, and Brian Marston have put considerable thought and research into the ecological value of salmon, other than for human consumption and sport. Their findings were published in "Fishes and the Forest" in the June 1998 issue of the journal *Bioscience*.

We were both curious about where adult salmon go in the winter. When Bob met William Pearcy, author of the book *Ocean Ecology of North Pacific Salmonids,* we knew we had to write about that topic.

Finally, the incident that prompted us to write about sand lance is described in the article itself; but

Cutthroat trout

it was our own observations and readings that led us to conclude that this little fish may be one of the most important fish in the North Pacific Ocean.

You can read more about the interesting behavior of fish in Bob's book *Alaska's Fish: A Guide to Selected Species*.

For natural history information on salmon and trout we recommend *Pacific Salmon Life Histories* edited by Groot and Margolis, and the book *Trout* edited by Stolz and Schnell.

Salmon
IN
WINTER

In summer, when five species of Pacific salmon return to Southeast waters to spawn, there's little question where adult fish of the *Oncorhynchus* (salmon) genus are. Most Southeasters have tracked them down to fill their frying pans, fish totes, or freezers. But by December the spawning runs have ended, and even most of the carcasses along rivers and stream banks have been cleaned up by bears, birds, and other agents of nature.

As winter closes in and the pace of life slackens, we might begin to wonder where the next generations of salmon are. Where are the fish that will flock homeward as spawners next year, or the year after, or the year after that?

Many are out in the Gulf of Alaska, where most salmon from Southeast Alaska go to grow from juveniles to adults.

All Southeast salmon hatch in fresh water. They spend varying amounts of time in fresh water, depending on their species. Then as juveniles they make their way to salt water. At that point, they range in size, again depending on species. Pink salmon are a little over an inch long. King salmon are about three inches long. And cohos are four to six inches long.

Once in salt water, the young fish may spend a few weeks in protected inlets, estuaries, and other nearshore waters feeding. However, by the end of June, most of them have moved to more open inside waters within Southeast Alaska.

Beginning in late July and August, these young salmon leave Southeast's inland waters and migrate to the Gulf of Alaska. For example, biologists have observed millions of juvenile pink salmon schooling up and

Coho salmon that return to Southeast rivers to spawn have spent about 18 months growing in the ocean.

migrating through saltwater passages, including Sumner Strait, Chatham Strait, Peril Strait, and an area between west Prince of Wales and Noyes islands. No doubt other species of salmon behave in a similar manner.

Life in the Gulf

Joined by their cohorts from streams on the outer coast, most of the youngsters spend several months along the Gulf of Alaska coast, migrating to the north and west along a narrow corridor about 18 to 25 miles wide. They're helped along by prevailing currents near the surface of the water. The Alaska Current, a branch of the Japanese or Kuroshio Current, flows north and west along Southeast and Southcentral Alaska and intensifies into the deep, westward Alaska Stream. Then prevailing currents cycle south and east, completing a great counterclockwise gyre that turns again toward the Alaska coast. During winter the Aleutian Low, an area of intense atmospheric low pressure over the Aleutian Islands, increases this huge oceanic circulation system.

Salmon usually swim in counterclockwise orbits in the same direction as the cyclonic gyres. Pinks, which feed in the ocean for only one year, generally make one orbit. Salmon that spend more years at sea make more orbits. Sockeye salmon appear to travel almost constantly during their ocean migrations and may cover as much as 2,300 miles in a year.

The Gulf of Alaska is very productive. Currents bring nutrient-rich water from deep in the ocean by a process called "upwelling," and winter storms help mix and disperse the water. Nitrogen and phosphorus, not depleted as they often are in surface waters, act much like fertilizer on a garden. They foster blooms of phytoplankton, tiny plants that drift in the ocean and provide the first link in the whole oceanic food chain—which includes free-swimming crustaceans, squids, fishes, and other creatures that salmon feed on.

Making their way through this oceanic smorgasbord, Southeast salmon grow to adulthood on the ocean's bounty. Depending on their species, they feed for various amounts of time in the ocean environment, achieving more than 95 percent of their growth while they are at sea.

• **King salmon** spend three to five winters, often doubling their weight each year.

In winter, salmon spawned in Southeast Alaska swim in counterclockwise orbits congruent with prevailing currents in the North Pacific Ocean. During their winters at sea, which number from one to five depending on their species and other factors, the fish attain their adult size and weight.

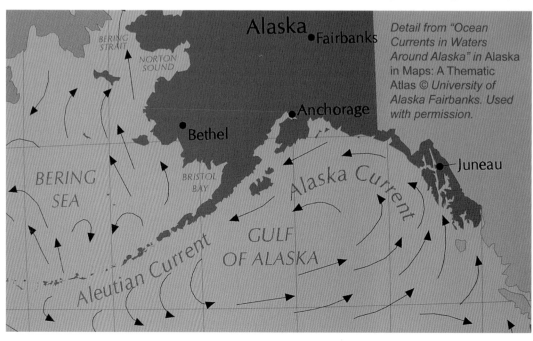

Detail from "Ocean Currents in Waters Around Alaska" in Alaska in Maps: A Thematic Atlas © University of Alaska Fairbanks. Used with permission.

When they return to fresh water to spawn, they weigh 10 to 50 pounds.

• **Sockeye salmon** usually spend two or three winters at sea and reach about four to eight pounds.

• **Chums** spend three to five winters. Full-grown adults weigh seven to 18 pounds.

• **Pinks** spend only one winter and grow to an average of about four pounds.

• **Cohos** spend only one winter at sea, too, but since they spawn in the fall, they have 18 months in the ocean to feed and grow. Full-grown adults usually weigh seven to 12 pounds.

Studies of salmon scales, which record growth much the way tree rings do, show that the fishes' growth slows in winter. It increases again by late February, as days get longer and food becomes more abundant.

In recent years salmon populations in the Gulf of Alaska have been the highest on record. In fall 1999 the Alaska Department of Fish and Game reported that an all-time high of 77 million pink salmon were taken commercially in Southeast, pushing the entire regional salmon catch to 95.5 million fish, also a record. The *Juneau Empire* reported there were so many fish that processors ran out of cans and stopped taking pinks, even though the fish continued to run strong into September.

Most researchers attribute the high populations primarily to warmer coastal sea temperatures following a major change in ocean conditions in 1976. These favorable conditions for Southeast salmon have continued, and the runs should remain strong for at least a few more years.

But a number of scientists are warning that the record salmon numbers since 1980 may be ending. In *Ocean Ecology of North Pacific Salmonids,* an excellent book about salmon in the ocean, William Pearcy suggests that the phenomenal increases in the Alaska salmon catch may be explained by increased survival coinciding with favorable ocean conditions, drastic reductions in the numbers of salmon intercepted by high seas fisheries (now illegal), and releases of juvenile hatchery fish, which now number more than five billion fish a year from Pacific Rim countries and states.

One disturbing trend is that fish of several salmon species seem to be getting smaller. Although Southeast's 1999 pink salmon catch set a record for numbers of fish, it did not set a corresponding record for weight. The average weight of pink salmon statewide was only 2.9 pounds, a full pound less than is considered normal. In similar findings, chum salmon studied at the head of Portland Canal in southern Southeast Alaska decreased 46 percent in weight between 1976 and 1991.

These trends could be the result of changes in oceanographic conditions, increased numbers of salmon released, or a combination of many factors. At any rate, change is underway in the ocean region where Southeast salmon do most of their growing, and for now no one is certain how it will affect future generations of fish that return to Southeast to spawn.

When coho salmon return to spawn after a year feeding in the Gulf of Alaska, they usually weigh between seven and 12 pounds.

Young coho salmon live in Southeast streams from one to four years before migrating to sea as smolts.

95

Life in Fresh Water

While Southeast's ocean voyaging salmon roam the North Pacific, some king salmon, and a few cohos spend the winter in inland salt waters. At the same time, in thousands of Southeast rivers, streams, and lakes, juvenile salmon in several different age groups are undergoing their earliest stages of growth. The youngest of these salmon are still eggs, deposited in the gravel and fertilized by spawning adults in the summer and fall.

The eggs of king salmon may be buried as much as two feet down. They are the largest of salmon eggs, and they require more oxygen than the eggs of other salmon, so rivers and streams suitable to support them are limited.

The eggs of pink salmon are usually buried between eight and 12 inches deep.

How long salmon eggs incubate in the gravel depends on both the species of salmon and water temperatures. The colder the temperature the slower the embryo will develop and the longer the time till hatching.

About a month after they were fertilized the eggs begin to "eye up," and the backbones and eyes of the tiny embryos become visible. About three months later, young salmon begin to hatch. The tiny fish, each with a yolk sac hanging from its abdomen, appear within the gravel, feeding on the nutrients within the egg sac.

Once the egg sac is used up, the young fish—by now about an inch long—emerge from the gravel, ready to take on a more challenging environment.

Southeast king salmon stay in their natal streams for one year after they emerge from the gravel. Cohos spend one to four years in their natal streams. Most Southeast chum and pink salmon move out to salt water within a few days after emerging from the gravel.

Sockeye salmon spawn mostly in streams associated with lakes and sometimes along lake shores, so their eggs may hatch during winter in any of these settings. Those emerging in streams migrate to lakes, where they live for one to two years.

So in winter Southeast Alaska streams and lakes may hold young salmon one to four years old and sometimes salmon of two species.

Surviving the winter is a challenge for young salmon. They must move away from areas of fresh water that might freeze. They must avoid being swept out of streams by winter floods. They must avoid predators such as mink, otter, and cutthroat trout at a time when their swimming ability is reduced because cold water temperatures lower their metabolic rate.

In winter young cohos move to the cover of logs, exposed tree roots, and undercut banks. Many seek out spring-fed tributaries and portions of streams where upwelling ground water keeps the stream from freezing. And the fierce territoriality they exhibit toward each other in summer decreases as they move closer together within suitable wintering areas.

At Hood Bay Creek on Admiralty Island, we observed large schools of young Dolly Varden and coho salmon moving upstream in the fall. Subsequent studies showed that these fish were seeking spring areas near the headwaters of the stream—the only significant parts of the stream that were ice-free during periods of extreme cold. •

From Egg to Fish in a Southeast Stream

These photos are of Dolly Varden, whose timing and development are similar to that of coho salmon. The colder the temperature of the water, the longer an embryo takes to develop and hatch.

1) In mid-October, on the day the egg is fertilized, first cell division occurs.

2) By the second day there are 16 cells.

3) 24 days later, in the second week of November, the optic lobes and skull development are visible.

4) After 81 days, in the first week of January, eyes and pectoral fins are visible. The embryo is about half an inch long.

5) Toward the end of February the embryo hatches. Living off its yolk sac, the young fish continues to develop in the gravel for another two months.

6) By the first of May the young fish emerges from the gravel and begins to feed on its own. It is about an inch long.

The Perfect Prey

Bob's Recollections

In May 1985 I was walking along the beach on north Douglas Island near Juneau when a small silvery fish about six inches long plummeted down out of the sky and hit the ground nearly at my feet. Startled, I looked up to see that a bald eagle flying overhead had dropped it. Luckily, I had my camera with me. I photographed the fish, then carried it back to the water and set it free. It was the first live Pacific sand lance I had ever seen. My curiosity about its ecology and behavior has led to some fascinating discoveries over the ensuing years. I've learned that the sand lance may be not only one of the most important fish in the North Pacific Ocean but also the oceanic version of "the perfect prey."

At night or when they are not feeding, Pacific sand lance burrow into the sand to conserve energy and escape from predators. This sand lance is just emerging from the sand under about three inches of water.

Sand lance are narrow, silver-sided fish usually six to eight inches long. They are shaped much like the long, steel-tipped spears carried by medieval knights, thus their common name sand "lance." They have a pointed snout and a lower jaw that projects beyond their upper jaw, making a nice tool for digging in the sand. A long dorsal fin extends along their backbone stopping just short of their forked tail. They look almost eel-like when they bend and curve their narrow bodies as they swim through the water or wriggle across the sand.

Sand lance are "forage fishes." Like Pacific herring, eulachon, and walleye pollock, they occur in great numbers and travel in schools, providing a major food source for other oceanic creatures such as salmon, seabirds, and marine mammals. In Southeast Alaska sand lance are the primary food of marbled murrelets, small, mottled brown seabirds commonly seen on the water.

At times sand lance make up more than 50 percent of the diet of arctic terns, horned and tufted puffins, common murres, pigeon guillemots, king and coho salmon, Pacific halibut, Dolly Varden, and several species

Richard MacIntosh

and sand lance have adopted a number of strategies to try to tip the scales toward survival in a fish-eat-fish world.

During the daytime when they are feeding, they swim through the water in what biologists call a "selfish herd." Crowding together in large schools, they present potential predators with a confusing sight—a wall of wiggling bodies with eyes peering out from all parts of it. This makes it difficult for predators such as murrelets to zone in and pursue a single fish, and each individual fish has a better chance of survival because one of the many other fish around it may end up as lunch while it swims free.

Black-legged kittiwakes are among a number of species that feed on sand lance in Southeast Alaska.

of rockfish in Southeast. Variations in the availability of sand lance greatly influence both the survival and the breeding success of many of these species.

Besides being abundant, sand lance have other qualities that make them particularly valuable as prey for seabirds. They are high in body fat during summer, so they make neat high energy food packages when birds such as arctic terns, puffins, and pigeon guillemots are trying to put on weight and feed their young. They're just about the right size for the birds to feed to their chicks, and their sleek, slender shape makes them easy for chicks to swallow.

A single two-ounce sand lance would provide little reward for a 250-pound harbor seal or a 30-ton humpback whale, but a closely-packed school of thousands of wriggling fish is a potential banquet. So schools of sand lance attract seals, and they make many a meal for Southeast's humpback whales, which may herd them together into a tight cluster by circling and blowing ever narrowing spirals of bubbles in the water before plunging upward to engulf a bathtub-size mass of closely-packed, squirming fish.

Serving as important prey is not a fate that most species of animals accept willingly,

What happens, though, is that murrelets often drive a whole school of fish toward the surface of the water, where they then become accessible to other predators that can't dive much below the surface after them.

In what can sometimes turn into a "feeding frenzy," large gulls land on the

A common raven feeds on a sand lance it has dug up.

Burrowing sand lance attract a flock of eagles and gulls on the Mendenhall Wetlands near Juneau airport.

water and jab at the fish. Arctic terns and Bonaparte gulls hover, then plunge into the water after them. Bald eagles swoop down and grab them in their talons by the fistful. And once again, the unfortunate sand lance become easy prey for other creatures feeding and nesting during Southeast's short, intense summer.

Sand lance face another disadvantage. Like bottom-dwelling fish such as sculpins and flatfish, sand lance do not have a swim bladder to give them natural buoyancy. Unless they swim constantly, they sink to the bottom. So at night, and at times during the day when they are not feeding, sand lance conserve energy and hide from predators by burying themselves in the sand.

One catch to the strategy of burrowing is that, not surprisingly, sand lance can burrow only in certain types of substrate, so they are crowded together into a few suitable locations.

In 1978 Edmund Hobson and Lou Barr from the National Marine Fisheries Service spent 10 days scuba diving to study sand lance in a cove at the head of Steamer Bay on Etolin Island, south of Wrangell. They found that during the day the sand lance swam out to the mouth of the cove and schooled up with Pacific herring to feed on tiny crustaceans carried by tidal currents. At night virtually all the sand lance in the cove burrowed down into the cove's only patch of loose, coarse sand. (Everywhere else in the cove the bottom was more silty or gravelly, or was made up of finer sand.)

Other studies have come up with similar findings: sand lance burrow in areas that are not muddy, silty, or rocky, and where the sand is well drained and not too tightly packed.

When sand lance bury themselves in shallow, intertidal areas, they can be exposed to air at extreme low tides. But the little fish seem to have physiological mechanisms to deal with that, since they can survive for at least five and a half hours in damp exposed sand. Exactly how they do this is not known. Perhaps they can somehow use oxygen from the air.

Even when they're buried, sand lance inevitably attract predators. In deep water, humpback whales may scuff the sea floor with their jaws to disturb sand lance and flush them out of hiding. At low tide when burrowing areas are exposed, ravens and crows dig for the little fish, scooping sand to the side with a twist of their heads.

In 1997 Mary Willson, then a research biologist at the Forest Service Pacific Northwest Research Station in Juneau, made further studies of sand lance at Mendenhall River and at Berners Bay north of Juneau. She discovered that ravens and crows could detect the buried sand lance at low tide and were quite successful at excavating them.

have declined, the fishing activity has moved lower and lower on the food chain.

Forage fish such as sand lance face increasing fishing pressure in a number of undeveloped countries, where they are harvested and shipped out to make food for farmed fish. This moves the nutrients and energy encompassed in massive quantities of forage fish out of local ecosystems, often depleting them and the crucial food supply for local people and wildlife.

If this were to happen in Alaska it could have devastating effects on the more than 100 species of wildlife that depend on the tiny sand lance for both survival and successful breeding and reproduction. The

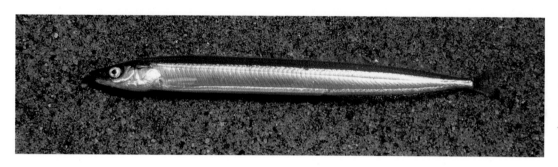

Adult sand lance are narrow, silver-sided fish about six to eight inches long.

She also found that ravens often carry sand lance to their nests in nearby forests, or store them in trees near the nest. So sand lance no doubt occasionally become food for other forest animals such as Steller's jays, shrews, and weasels.

Lou Barr, who is both a fishery biologist and commercial fisherman, told us of one bizarre instance when he found a fresh sand lance in the alpine while he was goat hunting above McGinnis Creek near Juneau. It had probably been dropped by an eagle or a raven.

Although they are edible (and some folks say quite tasty), sand lance are not usually human prey in Southeast Alaska. As times change, however, that, too, may change. On a worldwide scale, as major fish populations

same could happen if seabeds, tidal areas, or wetlands are developed or disturbed without consideration for those crucial areas where sand lance spawn and burrow for protection.

Much of the ocean life we depend on in Southeast and other parts of the North Pacific may rest on the slender back of a small, easily frightened fish that spends much of its time and energy trying to keep from being eaten.

AN AVIAN BANQUET

In 1987 my friend the late Pete Isleib of Juneau and I found a sand lance burrowing area on the Mendenhall Wetlands near the Juneau airport.

We were walking on the wetlands near Mendenhall River when we saw some 85 bald eagles feeding on something in a sandy area not far from the mouth of the river. Through a spotting scope we were able to see that the eagles were walking around and rapidly moving their feet up and down, almost as if they were dancing.

Hundreds of sand lance, apparently panicked by the activity, were popping up out of the sand and lying on the surface exhausted. (See photo above) The eagles were having a feast.

Several years later my friend Mary Willson and I went out and saw northwestern crows digging sand lance in the same area. They generally captured sand lance in eight digs or less. (See photo to left)

The Gifts of Salmon

The first decade of a new millennium is probably a good time to step back and whisper a word of thanks for some of the natural creatures and processes that underlie life for all of us here in the Panhandle of the Forty-Ninth State. If we were to hand out accolades, one of the biggest might go to salmon—the kings, cohos, sockeyes, chums, and pinks that are one of the most important resources in our Southeast region.

The Alaska Department of Fish and Game has identified more than 14,000 streams and 1,300 lakes that support salmon runs in Alaska, and there are probably many more. Southeast has its fair share—more than 400 lakes and 5,000 river and stream systems that produce salmon.

In 2002, commercial fisheries in Southeast Alaska harvested an estimated 57 million salmon, and fishermen received more than $50 million for their catch. Sport anglers in Southeast harvested about 458,000 salmon. Another 66,000 salmon were taken in Southeast for subsistence and personal use.

But salmon do more for us than provide food and income. According to a publication from the Pacific Northwest Research Station of the USDA Forest Service ("Fish and Forest: Ecological Links Between Water and

A bald eagle proclaims its ownership of a salmon carcass.

A common raven feeds on chum salmon carcasses.

Salmon and their scavengers knit together the ocean, fresh water, and the land.

streams. Since then, studies have shown that removing the Dollies did not benefit salmon populations. Instead we learned the Dollies may perform an important service.

When spawning salmon deposit their millions of eggs in stream bottoms, certain numbers of eggs always break free and drift away. Eggs deposited by early spawners also can be disturbed and washed free by later spawners. And during the critical months that eggs are incubating, storms and floods often wash great numbers of eggs out of the gravel where they'd been deposited.

Drifting eggs will not hatch, and when they die they can develop a fungus called *Saprolegnia* that can infect healthy salmon eggs in the gravel. Egg scavengers such as Dolly Varden, gulls, and sculpins help use an otherwise "wasted" resource and undoubtedly help prevent disease from infecting live eggs and killing them.

Land"), researchers are discovering a great deal about the way salmon knit together the ocean, fresh water, and the land. They distribute nutrients, promote the health and reproduction of other species, influence the winter survival of birds, mammals, and fish, and even affect vegetation along stream banks and in the forest.

Salmon not only feed saltwater species such as seabirds, seals, sea lions, porpoises, and orcas. More than 40 different species of animals forage on salmon in Southeast's fresh waters as well. They eat salmon eggs, juvenile fish, and live adult salmon or their carcasses.

American dippers, several species of gulls, rainbow and cutthroat trout, and Dolly Varden feed on the eggs released into streams and lakes by spawning salmon, but it took Alaskans a while to understand that. In the 1920s to '40s, for example, Dolly Varden were condemned as pernicious predators on salmon young and eggs, and for nearly 20 years the U.S. Bureau of Fisheries offered bounties of between two-and-a-half and five cents for Dolly Varden tails from Alaska

Fish-eating mergansers, kingfishers, and terns often nest in areas where they can feed on young salmon that have not yet gone to sea. Juvenile fish such as two-inch-long coho

salmon provide highly nutritious meals for these birds and their hungry chicks.

Bald eagles, bears, mink, and river otters feed on adult salmon and their carcasses when the adults return to Southeast rivers, streams, and lakes to spawn and then die. What's more, researchers are finding that the seasonal timing of the salmon runs is critical to the well-being and reproductive success of many animals.

Salmon return to their natal streams in late summer and fall—the time of year when bears must lay on fat to carry them through six or more months of winter hibernation. Female bears especially need to gain sufficient weight in order to reproduce and produce milk if cubs are born in the winter den. Hordes of returning salmon are a primary source of high quality food,

along a single stretch of river. Young bald eagles leave their nests at about the same time that pink salmon return to spawn in August, and the carcasses of salmon provide the immature birds with easily acquired food at a time when they are just learning to forage for themselves.

Along the Chilkat River a late fall run of chum salmon feeds thousands of eagles when food elsewhere is in short supply.

One of us experienced the importance of spawning salmon to mink at her cabin on Admiralty Island one September. When the pungent odor of dead fish prompted an inspection of the crawl space beneath the cabin, she excavated four and a half pink salmon carcasses that a mink had apparently dragged up from the beach and stashed in preparation for a delayed banquet.

Arctic terns often feed juvenile coho salmon to their young.

especially in the fat-rich eggs and brains that bears selectively eat when they capture live salmon or scavenge carcasses.

Returning salmon also attract crowds of gulls and sometimes hundreds of bald eagles

A study in the *Canadian Journal of Zoology* suggests that mink have delayed the timing of their breeding cycle so that females are lactating (a time of especially high energy cost) when salmon carcasses are available.

River otters and other carnivores are part of the food chain that links spawning salmon and other fish with healthy forests and wetlands.

In 1998, three ecologists from the Juneau Forestry Sciences Laboratory—Mary Willson, Scott Gende, and Brian Marston—described these and other important ways in which spawning salmon (and other seasonally spawning fish such as eulachon, Pacific herring, and sand lance) are important to the health and productivity of streams, lakes, and forests and the many species of wildlife that inhabit them.

Because salmon die when they spawn, they provide a tremendous influx of nutrients to spawning streams. The authors wrote:

Their carcasses accumulate in streams, where they are stranded in the shallows or caught on logs and rocks, or along lakeshores. A rich community of algae, fungi, and bacteria develops on the carcasses, and populations of invertebrates increase. These invertebrates then serve as food for fish in the stream, including juvenile salmon.

Stream invertebrates include mayflies, caddisflies, and stoneflies.

The three ecologists also described what they call 'the potential fertilizer effects of salmon carcasses on land':

Bears and other carnivores commonly haul salmon, living or dead, onto stream banks and back into the forest. Eagles sometimes move carcasses to the streamside, and ravens and crows cache salmon bits in trees and under grass and rocks. Decomposers then break down incompletely consumed carcasses and digested remains of fish in feces of vertebrate consumers.

In this way, nutrients from the sea pass from the bodies of salmon into the soil, near-stream vegetation, and animals within the forest.

Research results suggest that bird populations are denser on streams with salmon runs, and studies using isotopes as markers have traced nutrients from the bodies of dead salmon into the ecosystems along rivers. One study on the Snoqualmie River in Washington state found that salmon provided 18 percent of the nitrogen in streamside trees, 25 to 30 percent of the nitrogen and carbon found in insects, and 25 to 40 percent of the nitrogen and carbon in young salmon, which feed on the insects.

A study of phosphorus released from sockeye and pink salmon in the Karluk Lake system in southcentral Alaska measured amounts equivalent to the recommended application of a standard commercial fertilizer to evergreens and trees.

As the Juneau ecologists note, because nitrogen and phosphorus are often in short supply in Southeast environments, the addition of even small amounts of them can have large effects on productivity.

If salmon are even deeper at the heart of the Southeast landscape than we thought, and if quantities of fish and the timing of their arrival in spawning streams influence not only human harvests but the functioning of wildlife communities and the forest itself, people in Southeast Alaska have even more to consider in balancing decisions about fish, wildlife, and land uses. We are only beginning to understand the gifts of salmon that are integral to our lives here, it seems.

When we talked with Willson about what she and her colleagues found during their research, she said:

It's a whole network of interactions that ties land and sea together. Alaska may be the one place—other than Eastern Russia—where this reciprocal interchange between water and land is still happening on a large scale. It really enriches a walk through the woods to know about things like this—and to speculate about others. ●

Pioneers

The gifts of salmon are expanding! While environmental problems are driving wild salmon runs to extinction in the Pacific Northwest, new salmon runs are being created naturally in Alaska as glaciers retreat.

In Glacier Bay, scientists estimate more than 300 new streams have been formed within the last 200 years. About 60 percent of them are now believed to have salmon runs.

Mendenhall Lake, in front of Juneau's Mendenhall Glacier, did not exist 100 years ago when the glacier extended as much as two miles beyond its present location. Today the lake has populations of coho and sockeye salmon, and Steep Creek, which flows into the lake, has an impressive sockeye run.

According to Discovery Southeast naturalist Richard Carstensen, Steep Creek did not reach its present outlet on freshly deglaciated Mendenhall Lake until about 1955. It was probably sometime after that that sockeye salmon first colonized the area.

Nugget Creek falls, shown in the photo above, have recently been exposed by the retreat of Mendenhall Glacier.

WEIRD FISH

Humans often think of

fish as alien creatures, living underwater as we cannot, and looking and acting in ways that seem mightily strange to those of us who breathe air and live on land. But if we knew more about their lives, many kinds of fish might appear even weirder than we thought.

According to *Fishes of Alaska*, a total of 309 fish species from 76 families have been found in the waters of Southeast Alaska.

Many of their family names suggest how weird they seem to us. Ratfishes, spook-fishes, daggertooths, dreamers, tubesnouts, grunt sculpins, lumpsuckers, wolffishes, sand lance, and rag fishes—surely these are creatures both wondrous and strange.

Scuba diving is the best way to observe the greatest variety of weird fish in their natural habitat. Some are amazingly tame and divers actually touch and hand-feed them.

If you're less adventuresome, you can sit quietly near a tidal pool or turn over rocks to see shallow-water fish such as sculpins, gunnels, or pricklebacks. Aquariums in Southeast where weird fish are sometimes displayed include Auke Bay Biological Laboratory and DIPAC Hatchery in Juneau, and the hatchery at Sheldon Jackson College in Sitka.

Decorated Warbonnet

One of the weirdest piscatory disguises can be found on the *decorated warbonnet*. Members of the prickleback family, these cryptically colored fish look as if they have miniature forests of lichens growing on their heads. Among certain plants and coral, these fleshy flaps help make warbonnets virtually invisible to their predators and prey.

Grunt Sculpin

These active little saltwater fish, generally two to three inches long, can sometimes be seen in tide pools in Southeast Alaska, where they appear to jump and crawl about on the bottom.

Grunt sculpins get their name from the grunting and hissing sounds they make when they're removed from the water.

Female grunt sculpins also exhibit rather odd behavior: the female chases males until she traps one in a rock crevice, then she keeps him there until she lays her eggs. A grunt sculpin's eyes each operate independently, so

it can watch for danger or prey in two directions at once. In the photo above, the sculpin's left eye is looking backward.

Staghorn Sculpin

Like grunt sculpins, *staghorn sculpins* also make sounds — they hum when they're under stress. Try to take one off your hook and you may feel the vibration from the humming.

Staghorns are probably the most common of the weird fish that sport anglers catch, especially if the fisherman's bait nears the bottom. They're the ones many anglers call "double uglies," and they have sharp spines in their first dorsal fin and in "antlers" along the sides of their heads.

There are more species of sculpins in Southeast Alaska than of any other kind of fish—56 species in four families, to be exact. As with many of the other fish humans consider "weird," much of their "weirdness" stems from their remarkable and often complicated attempts at camouflage and disguise.

Buffalo Sculpin

Here's a fish that can look exactly like the rocks around it. If you look at one in an aquarium, with its irregular patches of dark brown, green-black, white, and purple, it looks less like a fish than like a rock with a mouth.

Pacific Spiny Lumpsucker

A *lumpsucker* can look like a reddish brown or pale green round rock complete with barnacles. But the spiny tubercles on its body are probably more useful in discouraging predators than for camouflage.

If a lumpsucker is attacked, it can inflate itself. This change in size and shape, along with the sharp spines, provides a substantial defense.

Lumpsuckers probably spend large amounts of time stuck to rocks and other objects using an adhesive disk on their bellies. The disk is actually modified fins.

Crescent Gunnel

These small, elongated fish look like eels, but they are not. They have a long dorsal fin that extends all the way back to the tail, where it merges with the tail fin, adding further to their eel-like appearance.

Gunnels are often found in tidepools filled with seaweed, where they hide under rocks encrusted with barnacles and other growth. They are an important food for fish-eating birds such as great blue herons and belted kingfishers.

Wolf-eel

Wolf-eels have sharp conical canine teeth for tearing and flat heavy molars for crunching. They can easily chomp through the hard shells of crabs, clams, and snails, and can deliver a serious bite to unwary humans.

This young eel in our photo is about two feet long, but adults can grow to six feet.

Dolly Varden

Even "common" fish sometimes exhibit behavior that humans consider weird. Some **Dolly Varden**, for example, engage in a practice known as "streaking." This seemingly odd behavior is an attempt by small, precocious males to outsmart larger spawning adults in producing the next generation. At the precise moment that large males and females are busy spawning—mouths agape, bodies quivering, sperm and eggs being extruded—the young males "streak" through, release their own sperm, and dart off.

THE WEIRDEST FISH OF ALL?

What's the weirdest fish in Southeast waters? It might be the **spotted ratfish**.

Ratfish look as if they were made up by a committee that could not agree. They are in the family Chimaeridae, named for the female monsters in Homer's *Iliad*.

The monsters are described as having a lion's forepart, a goat's middle, and a dragon's hind end; and the ratfish, too, appears to be made up of several different creatures. It has a large rabbit-like head, huge green eyes, forward-facing chisel-like teeth, and a body that tapers back to a remarkably long, rat-like tail, which accounts for its common name.

Ratfishes' behavior is about as weird as their looks. During elaborate courtship maneuvers, the males undergo striking changes in color. Later, females may take up to 30 hours to extrude their egg cases, which then hang from their bodies in a long filament for another four to six days.

Doug Wechsler

Male ratfish also have an unusual device called a *tenaculum* on their heads. They use this club-like appendage to grasp or stimulate the female during mating.

Ratfish can look pretty incongruous as they glide through the water like slow-flying birds by flapping their huge pectoral fins.

These fish are usually seen only by commercial fishermen, especially trawlers, and the occasional sport angler who accidentally snags one by one of those large fins. ●

Insects

Variable Darner

Queen bumblebee

Insects in Southeast Alaska

Insects are abundant and very important in Southeast Alaska. They feed our young salmon and trout in streams and lakes. They help pollinate the flowers we enjoy. They provide critical protein for many young birds and their parents. They help convert dead vegetation and carrion into nutrients that can be used by other plants and animals.

Most of us do not like certain insects. We especially do not like insects that bite us—mosquitoes, black flies, "no-see'ums," deer flies, and horseflies. In contrast with more northerly parts of Alaska, though, biting insects in Southeast are generally little more than an annoyance. Up north you may need head nets and special clothing to combat clouds of biting insects, but in most places in Southeast, occasional doses of insect repellent usually do the job.

Mosquito

Considerable attention has been given to the insects that harm and alter the forests in Alaska. We know, for example, that Southeast has a number of insects, such as the hemlock sawfly, that eat the leaves or needles of our trees. Others, like the spruce aphid, suck a tree's sap and reduce the tree's food supply. Still others such as bark beetles can cause widespread economic damage. Yet many insects are harmless (or beneficial), interesting, and even beautiful.

We started writing about dragonflies—which are indeed both interesting and beautiful—because we wanted to write an article about the Alaska State Insect. After interviewing John Hudson, we could not help but be caught up in his enthusiasm for these remarkable creatures. John suggested the theme for our article, "Living in Two Worlds," because that is what dragonflies do. We got so involved with "dragons" that John and Bob are now collaborating to produce a book on the dragonflies of Alaska.

The article on pollinators grew from our curiosity about what pollinates the first spring flowers that bloom when snow is still on the ground and there are few insects about. Our research led us into the fascinating adaptations that flowers have for attracting certain insects, and the numerous ways insects have evolved to take advantage of what flowers have to offer.

One book—*The Forgotten Pollinators*, by Stephen Buchmann and Gary Nabhan—really inspired us. It gave us a whole new perspective on how important insects are to all of us.

The article on beetles was prompted by a newspaper article we read about spruce bark beetle damage on the Kenai Peninsula. We wondered what effects this beetle had had on forests in Southeast Alaska and also where we could find some beetles and larvae to photograph. This led to an interview with Mark Schultz and Dustin Wittwer, two Alaskan experts on spruce bark beetles and, as it turned out, a great many other fascinating beetles as well.

Caddisfly

We especially appreciated the information in *Insects and Diseases in Alaskan Forests*, which Mark Schultz co-authored with three other scientists for the U.S. Forest Service.

Pollinators

In fall, as we enjoy pies and fresh jellies from the summer's berries, as we eat fresh vegetables from our gardens and harvest animals that make their living feeding on plants, we are indebted to a myriad of insects who performed valuable services during spring and summer. These are the pollinators—bees, flies, beetles, butterflies, and moths—who take pollen and nectar from flowers to feed themselves and their young, then end up carrying pollen grains from one flower to another.

Most of us take for granted the flowers and fruits that provide foods we eat (berries, zucchini, corn, wheat), products we use (cotton and many life-saving drugs), and natural wonders we enjoy (glowing fields of fireweed, leafy green skunk cabbage that feeds our deer, flowers in our gardens and public places). But we would have none of them without the natural process of pollination, in which pollen grains from the male parts of a flower are transferred to the female parts of the same flower or another flower.

Plants, unable to move around freely, face a challenge in transporting pollen from their male parts to their female parts so they can produce seeds for a new generation. An even greater challenge is to transport pollen from the male parts of one plant to the female parts of another. This *cross-pollination* produces offspring that are often larger and have more genetic variation—a benefit in coping with changes in the environment.

As plants have developed over time, many of them have devised ways to enlist

Hoverflies masquerade as bees, but they have shorter antennae and hold their wings out to the side when resting. They are often found on flowers with shallow blossoms, like this dandelion.

115

Queen bumblebees are especially important pollinators for early-blooming plants such as willows. This bee's entire body is covered with pollen grains that it will carry from blossom to blossom.

insects to provide the necessary transportation. They've developed showy blossoms, colorful petals, attractive shapes, and appealing odors to attract insects to come feed on their nectar and pollen.

Some plants, like the heart-leaved twayblade, an orchid described in the "Wild Orchids" section of this book, have developed rather specialized techniques. When an insect lands on a twayblade blossom, the flower blows its pollen out explosively, complete with a fluid that glues the pollen to the insect.

We have spent some time studying and photographing insect pollinators around Juneau, and we are fascinated by how various insects go about gathering their harvest—and how plants have evolved to help or hinder them. Here's some of what we've discovered.

Bumblebees

Bumblebees are important pollinators for a number of plants in Southeast. They are particularly important to many alpine plants because they are able to fly at low temperatures when most other insects are too chilled to be active. They are also important to plants at lower elevations.

Queen bumblebees, which winter over as adults, emerge in early spring before other pollinators such as flies and butterflies are around, so they are probably especially important to early-blooming plants such as early blueberry and purple mountain saxifrage. (See "The First Spring Flowers")

When queens begin their nests in underground cavities, they collect pollen in clumps and then lay eggs on the pollen for their first brood. When larvae emerge from the eggs, they feed on the pollen, which is rich in protein. Meanwhile, the adult bees eat mostly nectar, which is rich in energy-packed carbohydrates.

Bumblebees are particularly attracted to blue, irregularly-shaped flowers like lupines and beach peas. The bees are heavy enough to force open blossoms of vertically symmetrical blossoms like those of lupines, and their *proboscis,* or tube-like mouth parts, can reach deep into the base of a blossom where nectar is stored.

As the bees delve deep into a flower, pollen grains stick to the hairs on their bodies. The bees use their legs to comb the pollen into special storage sacs on their hind legs for carrying it back to the nest. But inevitably some pollen grains rub off the bees' bodies when they visit subsequent flowers, so the insects end up distributing pollen from the male part of a blossom to the female parts of other blossoms, achieving the pollination and cross-pollination that is so important to their plant hosts.

In his book on the natural history of the Cascade and Olympic areas of Washington state, Daniel Mathews describes the close relationship bumblebees have with monkshood, a blue- or purple-flowered plant commonly found in many parts of Southeast. He says that monkshood's odd-shaped flower excludes from its nectary all insects except "highly motivated, intelligent bumblebees"; and he notes that once bumblebees have been rewarded with monkshood nectar, they will tend to visit only monkshood blossoms.

Apparently this "loyalty" to a single type of flower benefits both the bees and the plants. Assuming it takes time and energy for a bee to learn how to extract nectar from a complex blossom, it would be to the bee's advantage to specialize in feeding on one species of flower rather than spending time and energy on learning how to deal with others. For the plant, on the other hand, pollen distribution would be more effective because the bees would carry pollen to other monkshood blossoms rather than to flowers of another species, where they would be of no help in producing a future generation.

Hoverflies

Some other important pollinators in Southeast look like bees, but they are actually flies in elaborate disguise. Hoverflies, or syrphid flies (members of the insect family Syrphidae, who often hover like helicopters) masquerade as bees or wasps, presumably as a way to discourage predators. They often have black and yellow bands, and some of them even buzz like bees and wasps. But they do not sting, and if you look closely you can distinguish them from bees and wasps

in three ways: They have only two wings, while bees and wasps have four. When at rest they hold their wings slightly out to the sides, while bees fold their wings over their backs. And their antennae are shorter than the length of their heads, while bees' antennae are longer than the length of their heads.

Flies are the most numerous and varied insect pollinators in Southeast.

Hoverflies have shorter mouth parts than bees, so they visit flowers with more shallow blossoms such as dandelions and daisies. They also eat mostly the protein-rich pollen, consuming only enough nectar to help dissolve the hard shells of the pollen grains. Still, their bodies brush against the blossoms as they eat, so they carry sticky pollen grains as they move from flower to flower.

Other Flies

Besides hoverflies, other varieties of flies are important pollinators. If you look at blossoms of plants such as cow parsnip in summer you will see flies of many different shapes, sizes, and colors feeding on the pollen and nectar. As they move about, of course, they carry pollen on their bodies from male parts of blossoms to female, and from flower to flower.

Flies, like beetles, may be attracted by carrion-like smells. In fact, we have noticed large numbers of flies on skunk cabbage blossoms at high elevations.

Though most of us think of mosquitoes as vicious predators out for blood, they are important pollinators, too—and the males do not even bite. As one of our sources noted, "Male mosquitoes drink only sugary fluids such as flower nectar. Since they vigorously probe the flowers of certain plants, and can distinguish between different types of sugars, they play a role in the pollination of certain plants."

Female mosquitoes also drink sugary fluids, but most of us get to know them shortly before or after they've mated, when they suddenly go looking for a blood meal to provide extra protein for their eggs.

Beetles

In terms of evolution, beetles may have been the earliest plant pollinators. They visit plants to feed on pollen, which besides protein includes a little starch, oil, and more vitamins and minerals than nectar does.

Beetles are clumsy fliers, so they often visit flowers on which many blossoms are clustered close together, such as Labrador tea and skunk cabbage.

Tiny black beetles of the species *Pelecomalius testaceum* are one of the primary pollinators of skunk cabbage. They climb back and forth over the closely packed male and female blossoms on the large central spike inside the "hood" of the skunk cabbage flower. They come to eat pollen, but as they do, they distribute grains that cling to their bodies as they wander among the male and female blossoms.

Beetles seem to be especially attracted to flowers that emit what to humans are unpleasant odors, similar to the odors of rotting fish, carrion, dung, or urine.

Beetles, such as the long-horned beetle shown below, eat protein-rich pollen. They are fairly clumsy fliers so to save energy they tend to visit flowers with clusters of blossoms, like this Labrador tea.

Margined whites are the most common butterflies in Southeast. They visit a wide variety of flowers, no doubt helping to pollinate them.

Many studies suggest that specific plant odors attract distinct species of beetle pollinators—a tactic plants would benefit from in the same way they benefit from bumblebees' "loyalty."

Our Seldom-Appreciated Benefactors

We have talked mostly about pollination of wildflowers in Southeast Alaska, but throughout the world insect pollinators are crucial to fruit and seed production in the plants upon which much of human society depends.

According to the U.S. Department of Agriculture, both wild and managed pollinators are disappearing at alarming rates because of habitat loss, pesticide poisoning, diseases, and pests.

The number of commercial bee colonies in the United States plummeted from 5.9 million in the late 1940s to 2.7 million in 1995. In 1994 and 2004 local bee shortages forced many California almond growers to import honeybees from other states. And recent monitoring of pumpkins in New York State showed their blossoms still laden with pollen five hours after they opened in the morning, long after they had typically been stripped of all pollen by bees in seasons past.

We know a number of Southeast Alaska gardeners who pollinate their outdoor plants using paintbrushes because they do not feel they can rely on pollinators to do the job naturally.

While we are far from many of the factors that threaten pollinators in other parts of the world—invasions by pests such as Africanized bees, extensive spraying of insecticides, and loss of habitat and host plants for pollinating insects—it would be good for us to recognize the importance of the role pollinating insects play in a thriving natural world. We can help assure their continuation by limiting our use of pesticides, including nectar and host plants for pollinators in our gardens, and purchasing organic produce grown with a recognition of how important insect pollinators are to our daily lives.

Plant Adaptations
for Pollination

Plants have developed a wide variety of methods to ensure pollination. Some, such as our Sitka spruce trees, rely on wind to transfer their pollen. Others such as columbine and paintbrush are especially adapted for pollination by hummingbirds. Aquatic plants often rely on water currents to distribute their pollen.

So insects are not the only pollinators, but they are by far the most important for the vast majority of plants in Southeast Alaska. And some plants have developed remarkably complex ways to take advantage of them.

Bog orchids, as we describe in the "Wild Orchids" section of this book, go to great lengths to deposit and affix pollen onto the insects they attract to visit them. Fern-leaved goldthread, a tiny evergreen plant commonly found in Southeast forests, also has an interesting adaptation for attracting pollinators.

Most flowers produce nectar in "nectaries" near the base of their petals. Fern-leaved goldthread stores its nectar in five or six separate nectaries, one on each of its five or six petals.

These nectar reservoirs are about one-third of the way up the petal from the base (See the round yellow-green "knobs" in the photo above). To get to them, insects often crawl over the blossom's pollen-laden anthers. Thus they pick up pollen and unsuspectingly carry it to other goldthread blossoms.

Shooting stars, shown in the lefthand photo above, have brilliant pink flowers with their petals swept backward and their anthers forming a sharp-pointed cone. In yet another kind of adaptation, shooting stars discharge their pollen in an explosive cloud when a bumblebee grasps their petals and vibrates its wings, producing a high-pitched buzz.

The buzz is produced as the bee vibrates its flight muscles at up to 300 cycles per second. The vibrations loosen the pollen from tiny pores in the blossom's tube-like anthers, dousing the bee so it will carry pollen to the next shooting star it visits. ●

Living in Two Worlds

Southeast Alaska has few, if any, legends of mystical dragons. But we do have dragonflies. Each summer, especially in July and August, we see them darting and swooping across meadows and ponds—masters of the air for the few brief weeks of their adult lives.

But dragonflies come from the water. From eggs laid in or very near to water, they hatch into larvae, and they spend the first years of their lives underwater in shallow ponds and lakes. They breathe through gills. They feed on aquatic insects, tadpoles, crustaceans, and small fish. And we hardly see them at all.

After one to four years (or longer, depending on the species and surrounding temperatures) the larvae mature. They climb out of the water, clinging tightly to vegetation or some other convenient surface. No longer creatures of water, they take in gulps of air, building up pressure that splits their larval skin. Head first they crawl out. Their wings expand as they are pumped full of blood. And their new exoskeletons gradually harden. Soon they take to the air, where they will spend days or weeks feeding before they are ready to mate.

Adult dragonflies are superb predators. They may capture and eat as many as 300 aphids, mosquitoes, and other insects in a day. It's no wonder they are so successful. With four large wings, each able to move independently, they can hover, swerve, stop, fly backwards, and reach speeds of up to 60

When they reach maturity, dragonfly larvae crawl out of the water and change into their adult form.

(Above) This four-spotted skimmer recently emerged from its larval skin. At this stage the dragonfly is very vulnerable. Its wings are delicate and it cannot fly.

(Top right) This American emerald shows the metallic green eyes characteristic of its family.

(Lower right) This Hudsonian whiteface is one of the most common small dragonflies in Southeast Alaska.

miles an hour. In flight they can open their long, spiny legs, forming a kind of basket in which to capture insects and hold them. They may perch to feed, or eat their prey while still airborne.

Dragonflies have large, compound eyes that take up about two-thirds of their heads. With some 30,000 facets on each eye, the insect can see in many different directions.

Sidney Dunkle notes in his fascinating book *Dragonflies Through Binoculars* that:

Dragonflies can see all the colors we can see, plus ultraviolet light and polarized light, and can detect the flickering of light at twice the rate we can . . . Presumably, they use these abilities to see ultraviolet color patterns invisible to us, navigate by the pattern of polarized light in the sky, and see the pattern on fast-beating wings.

To learn more about dragonflies we interviewed John Hudson, a biologist in Juneau who studies and collects dragonflies.

Hudson has been studying dragonflies since 1995. "My dad is an entomologist," he said. "I got started with my first insect collection when I was six. I've always enjoyed collecting insects. Now I'm documenting what species of dragonflies are found in Alaska."

"Our weather is not conducive to dragonflies," Hudson told us. "Down South most dragonflies don't even fly if the sun's not out. Here in Southeast if they hunted only in sunshine they'd starve to death." Hudson said 18 species of dragonflies occur in Southeast Alaska. They include a number of **darners,** the largest and most conspicuous dragonflies. Some darners, like the lake darner, can be more than three inches long. The long, slender abdomens characteristic of darners earned them the nickname "devil's darning needle" because it was believed they sewed shut the lips of naughty children as they slept.

Darners are especially fun to watch. We recall watching one group of them gliding back and forth across a beach meadow, darting up and down, forward and back, as they captured small insects on the wing. Female darners insert their eggs into plant stems with the aid of special serrated appendages they use to saw holes in sedges, then lay their eggs in them, above or below the water.

Some other dragonflies you'll see in Southeast are **skimmers,** relatively small dragonflies that may have colorful markings like the Hudsonian whiteface or the crimson-ringed whiteface. Female skimmers typically dab their abdomens in the water to deposit their eggs, while their mates hover and guard them from other males. In some species males lead the females around while

When a dragonfly larva transforms into an adult, its old exoskeleton is left behind. These discarded "shells" can help identify the species of dragonflies found in an area.

John Hudson points out features of a sedge darner he has captured.

(Above) Damselflies, generally smaller and more delicate than dragonflies, are classified as a suborder (Zygoptera) of dragonflies (Odonata, or "the toothed ones"). Damselflies at rest usually hold their wings together over their backs rather than outspread as dragonflies do. These northern bluets are mating in the "wheel position" that is typical of both dragonflies and damselflies.

(Above right) Subarctic darners, nearly three inches long, may feed on meadow-hawks, which are about half their size.

they lay their eggs, or lower the female into the water.

Hudson said **emeralds,** of which we have several species in Southeast, are his favorites. "Emeralds are not that common," he said. "They breed in bogs and fens and come out for only short periods during the day. But the *color!* They exude a green wax, and have metallic green bodies and eyes. These insects are rare and exciting—like finding gold."

Not until Hudson showed us some of the dragonflies he has collected did we realize how much dragonflies can vary in size, color, and stoutness. Hudson showed us how many of them have remarkable color patches and patterns on their bodies—characteristics that can be used to identify their species. Intricate patterns in their wings can also be useful in identifying species.

Hudson has sent a number of specimens to Dennis Paulson at the University of Puget Sound, who published a *Field Key to Adult Alaska Dragonflies.* Two were new

records, species not previously reported in Southeast Alaska. One was a crimson-ringed whiteface, a skimmer that Hudson found on South Prince of Wales Island in 1997. The other was a Whitehouse's emerald found in a bog near Juneau in 2003.

But collecting and identifying species is only part of the story, Hudson said. We also need to understand the role of dragonflies in the food web. "Dragonflies are fierce predators in both the nymph and the adult stage," he said. "But they are also prey. The larvae are eaten by fish. The adults are eaten by birds such as kingfishers, kestrels, northern shrikes, and small hawks."

Smaller species may even be eaten by the tiny carnivorous sundew plants found in Southeast muskegs, he said.

"While strolling through muskegs in search of dragons, I've often heard the rapid wingbeats of black meadowhawks coming from the ground," Hudson told us. "Looking down one can find the little dragonflies fighting to lift themselves from the sticky hairs of the plant. They will probably be the only meal a sundew needs for a year."

Hudson said identifying species is important for other reasons as well. "Dragonflies can be very susceptible to environmental change," he said. "If water quality deteriorates, the abundance of their prey would be affected. . . . If climate change becomes an important factor in insect distribution, knowing where species occur now can help us understand what is happening.

"Adult dragonflies can be found anywhere, regardless of whether there's water," Hudson added. "They can catch mosquitoes and other prey just about anywhere. But when they're ready to mate, they have to meet up again near water to lay their eggs."

And that's where most of us see them—colorful reminders that, for some animals the worlds of air and water are not so far apart after all.

Alaska's State Insect

The four-spotted skimmer (*Libellula quadrimaculata*) is Alaska's State Insect. It was selected in a contest among school children throughout Alaska, and it beat out the bumblebee, the mourning cloak butterfly, and—yes—the mosquito. The Alaska State Legislature made the title official on August 24, 1995.

The four-spotted skimmer is found in most parts of Alaska, including Southeast and the Interior as far north as Fairbanks. Nearly two inches long, it is gray-brown and hairy, with (actually six) black spots, two at the base of the rear wings and four at nodes on all four wings.

John Hudson, who studies dragonflies in Southeast Alaska told us, "Four-spotted skimmers are the only species I know of that you can hold in your hand and feed." He recalls capturing some of the fast-fliers near Dredge Lake in Juneau." I held some small black flies in front of them," he said, "and they would reduce those flies to nothing."

Hmm. . . m . . efficiency. Isn't that an Alaskan characteristic?

Predators in the Ponds

1) The dragonfly larvae found in many Southeast lakes and ponds often attack prey much larger than themselves. The larva to the left (about one and a half inches long) is stalking a small three-spined stickleback.

2) (Right) The larva has now attacked the stickleback. It shot a jet of water out its back end to push itself forward, and simultaneously snapped out its large lower lip, which ends with a pair of sharp pincers but folds up under the larva's chin when not in use. The stickleback managed to dodge the attack and escape.

3) The larva to the left (a different one) was more successful. It has captured and is feeding on a stickleback.

WHEN PREDATORS BECOME PREY

(Left) An adult spreadwing is providing food for a predatory water strider. Holding the dragonfly with its two short front legs, the water strider will jab the insect with four needle-like mouth parts, injecting salivary fluid that will dissolve the dragonfly's insides. The strider will then suck them out, leaving the exterior skeleton behind.

(Right) An adult Hudsonian whiteface has been caught in a spider web and wrapped in silk to be consumed at the spider's convenience.

(Right) This Hudsonian whiteface, about 1.2 inches long, is caught in the sticky fluid exuded by glandular stalks on the leaves of round-leaved sundew plants. Normally sundews capture small flies such as mosquitoes, midges, and gnats, but the dragonfly will make a much larger meal.

Soon the plants' sticky stalks will bend inward, carrying parts of the dragonfly toward the centers of the leaves, which will exude digestive enzymes. Nitrogen and other nutrients extracted from the dragonfly will help the sundews survive in the nutrient-poor soil of an alpine bog. ●

127

The Good,
the Bad, and the Beautiful

Beetles in Southeast Alaska

"The Beautiful." This brilliantly colored net-winged beetle, about an inch long, is commonly seen in Southeast. Its bright colors probably signal potential predators that it is toxic or distasteful.

Beetles are the largest group of animals in the world. They represent one-fifth of all living organisms known to date, and they are amazingly diverse. They live in polar regions and rain forests, in deep caves and underwater. Scientists have described some 350,000 species of beetles so far, and more are being discovered every year.

We wondered if we might be missing something by knowing so little about these unobtrusive fellow residents of our region, so we gathered a few photos and stories about them. And we interviewed two biologists at the USDA Forest Service Pacific Northwest Research Station in Juneau who know a lot about beetles, especially in Southeast forests: Mark Schultz, Southeast Alaska entomologist, and Dustin Wittwer, biological technician and aerial survey coordinator for Alaska.

The Good
Beetles are pollinators, "decomposers," food for birds, and predators on many insects that humans consider pests.

Perhaps beetles' most important contribution to the world is as pollinators. According to *The Forgotten Pollinators* by Stephen L. Buchmann and Gary Paul Nabhan, beetles are pollinators for more than 80 percent of all flowering plants. That's many times more than estimates for bees, butterflies and other insects, or birds, bats, or wind.

Beetle pollinators in Southeast Alaska include *Pelecomalius testaceum,* the tiny black beetles believed to be the primary pollinators of skunk cabbage, and the larger long-horned beetle that we photographed on a blossom of Labrador tea. (See the story in this book describing "Pollinators.")

Mark Schultz reminded us that many beetles are also important "decomposers." Though humans may consider them bad, they help break down wood and plant material, releasing nutrients to the soil.

Round-headed wood-boring beetles, though sometimes serious pests in lumber and harvested logs, are probably among the most prominent insects involved in decomposing logging slash, stumps, and dead and dying trees in Southeast forests. These beetles bore into dead or dying trees and feed on them. Sometimes they also introduce or pave the way for conks and other wood-decaying fungi that continue the process of breaking wood tissue into nutrients that eventually will support new forest growth.

Ambrosia beetles, which bore into stumps and fallen or broken trees, take an even more creative approach. They are less interested in feeding on the host tree than in "gardening" fungi that they carry in to feed their larvae. The adult beetles excavate long, branching tunnels, or "galleries" into the heartwood and sapwood of host trees and "plant" spores of fungi that then grow in the galleries. After eggs are planted in shorter, nursery tunnels, the beetles stuff these "cradles" with fungus to feed the emerging larvae.

Schultz said one beetle he finds particularly interesting is the carrion beetle, which lays its eggs in salmon carcasses. "They're fairly good-sized," he said, "—about one centimeter wide and one and a half centimeters long—and they're very protective of their young. They'll keep other insects off the carcass.... And if they happen to fly into your house you can tell where they've been. They really smell like rotten salmon."

Beetles provide food for other animals in Southeast ecosystems. Woodpeckers love beetles and are well equipped to pry them out of cracks and holes in trees with their strong beaks. They can even home in on the sound of beetles chewing inside a tree.

Schultz believes beetles are an important food for most birds in Southeast. "Birds need protein to fledge their young," he said, "and insects are a good source of it. Beetles are slow, clumsy fliers, so they're probably relatively easy for birds to catch.... They're so abundant, they must be important."

Wittwer said that beetles probably make good fish food. If they are plentiful on trees

"The Good." Tiny beetles officially known as Pelecomalius testaceum *are important pollinators for skunk cabbage in Southeast Alaska.*

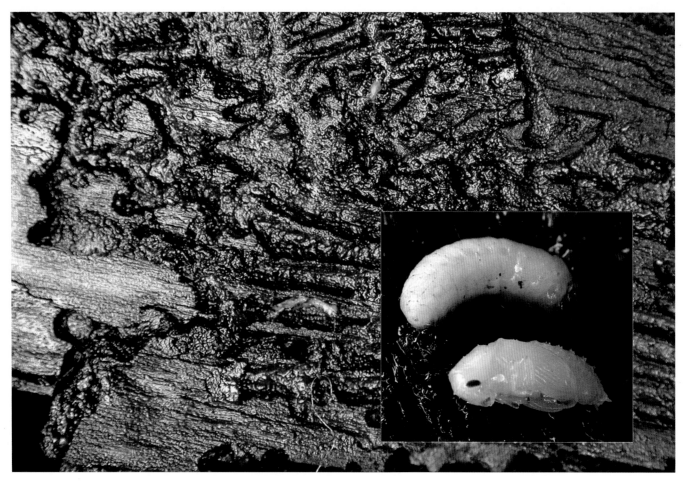

and bushes near rivers and streams, and they fall into the water, they would add to the food supply for young salmon and other fish, although no exact numbers have yet been researched.

Certain beetles are probably also considered "good" in human terms because they feed on insects that we consider pests—like the ladybird beetles some Southeast gardeners use to help control aphids.

If there's a "villain" in the Southeast beetle world it's probably the spruce bark beetle, though this tree-killer is not as serious

The Bad
Some beetles kill trees, destroy lumber, and infest food, art works, and other valuables.

a problem here as it has been in southcentral Alaska.

The spruce beetle outbreak on the Kenai Peninsula that began around 1990 has been

called "the largest single area of tree death caused by insects in the history of North America" by Glenn Juday, a forestry professor at the University of Alaska Fairbanks. The outbreak left some four million acres of mostly hybrid white and Sitka spruce dead or dying. Southeast Alaska has had no infestations on a similar scale.

Spruce beetles are always in the forest in low numbers, Schultz told us. They generally subsist in fallen or injured trees. But when environmental factors trigger a population increase, the beetles may have enough numbers to overcome healthy trees that are stressed.

That is what many researchers believe caused the bark beetle outbreak on the Kenai Peninsula. Annual temperatures there have increased three to five degrees Fahrenheit in the last 40 years, and there has been a long-running drought. Warmer summer temperatures may have sped up the spruce beetle's life cycle so larvae matured in one

"The Bad." Mark Schultz directed us to spruce beetle activity on a downed tree in Juneau's Mendenhall Valley. We could see the "galleries" the beetles had bored under the bark. Spruce beetle larvae (like the top creature in the inset) may survive in the tree for up to two years. Pupae (like the lower creature in the inset) are quiescent (inactive).

year instead of two; and the cold winters that might otherwise have knocked population numbers down failed to materialize.

"It's generally cooler and wetter here in Southeast, so that slows down the beetles' generational cycle" to two or three years, Schultz told us. He also said that the species of spruce beetles that overtook trees on the Kenai seem to like Sitka spruce, the predominant species in Southeast forests, far less than the white and black spruce found farther north.

Still, the Forest Service has been tracking small infestations of spruce bark beetles in Southeast for a number of years, Schultz said. That included small outbreaks near Taku River, Haines, Glacier Bay, the Stikine Delta, and Lituya Bay.

The latest data from aerial surveys showed only about 335 acres of spruce beetle activity in 2002, and 227 acres in 2003. That's far less than the 950 acres found in 2001, and a high of 35,700 acres of activity in 1996.

Schultz also told us about the fascinating life cycle of the spruce beetles found in Southeast Alaska, and gave us copies of the book *Insects and Diseases of Alaskan Forests,* which he and a number of other Forest Service specialists recently updated for distribution by the Forest Service Alaska Regional office. It's quite a story.

Beginning in late May and early June, as temperatures warm, adult spruce beetles emerge from infested trees and set out in search of new places to populate. Females lead the way, flying as much as seven miles or more to find new host trees. Spruce beetles prefer fallen trees, but apparently they repeatedly "test" standing trees to see if they can establish themselves inside them. Their goal is to bore through the outer bark and settle between the inner bark and the wood. They can feed on sugars that are stored there, and predators such as birds will find it difficult to get at the beetle young.

If the tree a beetle attacks is healthy, it will expel resin and other compounds to push the beetle out of the hole through which it entered, often with enough force to create a whitish or translucent globule of resin that can be seen afterwards on the tree. But if a tree is stressed by, say, injury or unusually warm or dry weather, it may be too weak to repel the beetle's invasion.

If a female beetle succeeds in settling into her chosen area, she will release pheromones, chemical substances that stimulate other beetles to join her in what Schultz called

an "aggregation." Females then construct "nuptial chambers" within the tree, attracting males with which to mate, and then laying their eggs. When the eggs hatch into larvae, the larvae in turn bore through the wood, creating winding tunnels, or "galleries," from which they can sense somehow which way to move without bumping into each other. Eventually the larvae mature into pupae, the final quiescent stage before adulthood.

Besides spruce beetles, Schultz described other beetles that can have negative impacts in Southeast. Cottonwood leaf beetles feed on tender shoots and chew holes in the leaves, not usually killing trees but slowing their

"The Bad." Leaf beetle larvae first skeletonize and later chew holes in the leaves of alder, willows, and cottonwood.

"The Beautiful." Predacious diving beetles, one of the largest groups of aquatic beetles in the world, are often very colorful. They consume large quantities of other insects, as both larvae and adults. Adults breathe by means of air bubbles trapped beneath their wing covers.

"Beautiful," too. This beetle, which we did not identify, has bright iridescent colors and delicate markings on its head and body.

growth. Powder post beetles often emerge from finished wood, such as picture frames or art objects, leaving tiny holes as they depart to complete their life cycle as adults.

Dermestid beetles chew on wool, leather, insect collections, and museum artifacts. And, of course, many of us have encountered unwelcome beetles in flour or bulk orders of grain or dogfood.

"We worry about beetles that come into Southeast" from other places, Schultz said. "Lots of them come in as larvae then mature as adults after they arrive." Many parts of the U.S. are fighting invaders of many kinds, including the Asian long-horned beetle, which kills hardwood trees. But so far no invasive beetles have become established in Southeast.

Beauty, of course, is in the eye of the beholder. But it didn't take too much effort for us to appreciate the remarkable shapes, colors, and beautifully formed appendages of the

The Beautiful
And then there are the pretty ones!

beetles we saw in our travels and in the collection Schultz and Wittwer helped assemble at the Forest Service Laboratory in Juneau.

Many beetles have iridescent colors and subtle markings on their heads and bodies, and their head shapes show great variety.

Beetles are indeed remarkable, and we know that even those humans consider "bad" or "ugly" may have useful roles in our Southeast ecosystems.

So keep your eyes open as you look amid moss or decaying wood (but hopefully not in your flour or the timbers of your house or cabin). Perhaps you, too, will enjoy these remarkable fellow residents, and eventually we will all know a little more about these lesser-known members of Southeast Alaska's natural world. ●

Mammals

Hoary Marmot

Mammals in Southeast Alaska

Muskrat

Southeast Alaska is one of the few places left in the world where many mammals roam freely and are not confined to parks. We have each lived on Admiralty Island, where we've had almost daily sightings of brown bears and frequent sightings of Sitka black-tailed deer, mink, and sometimes martens. When we take our skiffs salmon fishing we almost always see humpback whales, porpoises, harbor seals, and Steller sea lions.

Even from the Juneau road system you can see humpback whales, sea lions, seals, deer, mountain goats, black bears, river otters, beavers, mink, and weasels. Along hiking trails we have heard wolves howling, and once when anchored in a quiet cove, Marge and her partner Tom watched a wolf pack with pups romping on the beach. Brown bears have left claw marks and tufts of fur on our cabins, and on two occasions black bears tried to invade Bob's home late at night by pushing against the door and even turning the doorknob with their mouth. As Bob notes in his Recollection "Raven, the Mice, and the Weasel," a few mammals even tried to move in with him.

All in all 78 species of mammals have been documented for Southeast Alaska. The largest group (20 species) are rodents such as the Keen's mouse, hoary marmot, and muskrat. We have a surprising number of cetaceans (19 species) including the gray whale, sperm whale, and Dall's porpoise. And we have 14 species of carnivores, including the coyote, wolf, harbor seal, and wolverine. Mammals introduced to Southeast include the Norway rat, house mouse, raccoon, and elk.

Neither of us has gotten over the thrill of seeing large mammals like brown bears or breaching humpbacks, but we do not feature them in this book. Instead we focus on a few smaller creatures that attracted our attention—deer mice, squirrels, and porcupines. We didn't ignore what some have dubbed "charismatic megafauna," however. We wrote about hibernating bears (as well as marmots and ground squirrels) in "Chilling Out During Southeast Winters," and described the fate of humpback whales and sea otters in "Extinction: A Fate Worse Than Death."

We wrote the article on deer mice ("Keen Critter in Southeast") because their importance as food intrigued us when we wrote about owls. Things got especially interesting when Tom Hanley from the Forest Service Research Laboratory in Juneau generously shared his research into habitat use and food preferences of deer mice in Southeast.

"Nuts About Truffles" started when Bob found a couple of truffles obviously placed on top of a large bracket fungus by some creature in the woods. We sent the truffles to Gary Laursen at the University of Alaska in Fairbanks, who told us what species they were and a little about them. The more we researched the literature, the more we realized their importance, not only as food for flying squirrels but also for their role as mycorrhizal fungi in the forest.

Porcupines are one of the most easily observed mammals in Southeast. Because we'd both had several interesting experiences with them, we decided to write "A Prickly Tale" in the form of a story covering a yearly cycle. Uldis Rose's excellent book *The North American Porcupine* was a wonderful source for research findings and facts about porcupines' natural history.

The authority on the distribution of mammals in Southeast is *The Mammal Fauna of Southeast Alaska* by S.O. MacDonald and Joseph A. Cook, published by the University of Alaska Museum in Fairbanks. For interesting and engaging facts about Southeast's mammals we recommend *The Nature of Southeast Alaska* by Rita O'Clair, Robert Armstrong, and Richard Carstensen.

Sitka black-tailed deer

A Prickly Tale

On a drizzly morning in May a five-year-old female porcupine gives birth in the hollow of a tree somewhere in Southeast Alaska. Her newborn—also a female—is about 10 inches long and weighs about a pound. The young porcupine is quite well developed. Her eyes are open, and tiny teeth have already emerged. Except on her belly, she is covered with dense black hair. Amid the hair are soft barbless quills that will harden and begin to provide defense against predators within about an hour. But for now the young porcupine is hungry. She nurses for about 30 minutes, then curls up and falls asleep.

For several weeks before the birth the mother porcupine has been eating the newly emerging vegetation of spring—salmon-berry shoots, violets, marsh marigold, horsetails, and twisted stalk. Already she is regaining some of the weight she lost during winter, when she lived on the needles of Sitka spruce and inner bark of hemlock trees—less nourishing and more difficult to digest than the foods available in summer.

She has been pregnant for 217 days (about seven months), since mating with a large male in October. She will nurse her newborn for three and one-half months, until mid- or late August, while the youngster gradually learns to find and select nutritious leaves and other vegetation on her own. Female porcupines produce a single offspring nearly every year, and they invest considerable time and effort to bring a youngster to maturity.

This porcupine, with its aura of bright quills, was photographed in the subalpine area of Mt. Roberts near Juneau.

In summer porcupines often climb willows to feed on fresh, young leaves.

Early July

In the full flush of summer, the female porcupine has climbed about 10 feet up into a gangly Sitka alder shrub. She is stripping leaves from its outermost branches. Her daughter, not yet able to climb trees very well, is hiding in a tangle of brush a short distance away.

The adult female clings to the narrow branch, holding tight with her strong thigh muscles. She reaches her forepaws toward the outermost branch tip and strips its leaves with her long, curved claws. She seems ravenous, stuffing leaves into her mouth and chewing furiously. She's harvesting the newest and some of the tastiest and most nutritious growth on the tree.

The female's fur is thick and brownish-black with long, single guard hairs that stick out past the rest of the pelt. Amid the fur lie an estimated 30,000 quills—dangerous white needles with black tips. They protect every part of her body except the underparts, muzzle, and ears. Even if some are expelled against a predator, they will grow back in a matter of days.

Today it is the quills themselves that have attracted potential predators. Two women have spotted the porcupine in the tree and hope to gather quills to make jewelry. As they scramble through the brush to the base of the small tree, the porcupine hunches against the branch. Her quills spring up and fan out, their barbed tips pointing in every direction. She shivers, then closes her jaws, and her teeth make a chattering sound; she emits a strongly repellent smell.

Still, one of the women begins to climb the flimsy tree, reaching toward the porky with a long-handled broom wrapped with a towel. Branches sway precariously, and the porky shifts her weight, balancing with her broad, club-shaped tail. The woman gets closer.

Whomp! Before the broom can touch her, the porcupine flings her tail to the side and delivers a powerful blow. The shrub sways back and forth wildly, and the startled woman slips and falls several feet to the ground.

"Yikes, what a whap! Who'd think a little guy like that would be so strong?" she says to her companion. She looks at the 30 to 40 quills embedded in the towel-covered broom. "I think this'd better be enough. We'll really be in trouble if that thing falls down on us!"

The women leave, and the female porcupine eventually lowers her quills and continues feeding. Toward evening she will climb down to be reunited with her daughter. They are constant companions now, but gradually they will become less so. By October, her

daughter will be capable of climbing and feeding herself, and she'll probably wander off on her own.

Mid-October

The adult female, approaching estrus, is leaving a scent trail wherever she goes. That has attracted three males as suitors, and they fight among themselves to win her affections. Their combat is vicious. Even the large, winning male ends up bedraggled and carrying several of his rivals' quills.

The female waddles into dense underbrush, and the winning male pursues her in earnest. Whenever he approaches too close, she howls, making a sound like a cat yowling or a baby crying. She has complete control over this prickly courtship, and will move her heavily quilled tail to allow intimate contact only when she is ready for mating.

January

Back from the mouth of a river, overlooking half-frozen sloughs and tidal flats that spread out for half a mile, clusters of tall Sitka spruce and western hemlock line the steep bank. Two medium-sized spruce trees stand out from the others because of their odd, sparse silhouettes. In the top third of the trees, many branches are lacking needles and lateral twigs. The uppermost branches are virtually naked. Amid their lush neighbors, these trees look like bottle brushes worn down from overly conscientious scrubbing.

The cause of their distress—the female porcupine—has returned for a second year of feeding in the trees. Against the bright backdrop of a winter sky she is a dark lump that moves slowly up and down the tree. She has spread all four limbs around the trunk, using all the special features porcupines have developed for climbing. Her sharp claws dig into the bark, and the nubby, rubbery surfaces of her palms and the soles of her feet create friction for grasping the trunk.

She uses her tail as a brace. When she is climbing up, she uses the stiff, backward-pointing bristles on its underside to keep from sliding down. When she is climbing down, she can lift the tail then lower it at each claw-hold to test the way below. Her belly, unquilled, slides easily against the trunk as she moves, and her unfurred soles and palms allow her to feel the contours of the tree as she navigates.

Porcupines at lower elevations may feed on beach greens and other coastal vegetation.

(Below) Porcupines in Southeast Alaska are quite active during winter. Though they may shelter in dens during heavy snow or cold spells, they come out regularly, leaving footprints and traces of their swishing tails in the snow.

On the trunk the female strips off slices of bark, using at first the four curved incisors at the front of her mouth. These sharp teeth, covered with bright orange enamel that hardens them, are continually sharpened by scraping and their movement against each other. They grow continuously from deep inside the porcupine's jaws. The porcupine can actually close her lips behind them while rasping off tough outer bark from the tree, which she will not eat. She is instead after the tender inner bark, which she will take into her mouth, grind with her cheek teeth, then swallow. Special bacteria in her gut will help with the long, difficult process of digesting her food.

The female also ventures out onto branches, attracted by needles and the thin bark on young twigs. But she weighs 14 pounds, and as she moves farther and farther from the trunk, the smaller branches bend precariously, waving up and down from the weight of her body.

As if this is not frightening enough, at one point she stretches from one slender branch to the one above it, perhaps trying to save the effort of crawling all the way back to the trunk. Her whole body tips and sways as she grasps the upper branch with first one forepaw and then the other. But once she gets that far she cannot seem to let go with her two back legs. When she finally does, she dangles by her front legs, and hangs, swinging, with all four legs wrapped around the slender top branch.

The female may indeed be in a position as tenuous as it looks. Porcupines often fall, sometimes with dire results. Researcher Uldis Roze found porcupines in New York state with evidence of cracked skulls, fractured legs, and cracked hips, all apparently from falls. When he studied museum specimens to check for evidence of falls, he found more

than a third of the specimens showed healed fractures, some of which surely disabled their victims, at least to some extent.

But this time the female does not fall. She painstakingly jimmies herself back toward the trunk where the branch is more stable.

Meanwhile, the pale winter sun reveals a second porcupine, smaller, in a nearby tree, but nowhere near as high up as the female is. Apparently her daughter did not move as far from her mother as we had thought. She is still less than a year old; yet despite their proximity she's the porcupine equivalent of "grown up," and she's on her own.

In winter porcupines feed on the needles and cambium of spruce trees.

Porcupines, People, and Forests

One characteristic of porcupines often brings them into confrontations with humans. That is their lust for salt.

Like other herbivores, porcupines seldom get adequate sodium from their purely vegetarian diet. Yet sodium is essential to the functioning of nerve and muscle cells. That's why, especially in spring,

the numbers of road-killed porcupines along near-city highways dramatically escalate, and porcupines often approach homes, camping areas, and other human habitations, particularly at night.

As some unhappy homeowners and campers have discovered, porcupines crave salt so strongly they will gnaw on plywood (which is cured with sodium nitrate), axe and other tool handles impregnated with sweat, pack straps, hiking boots, painted signs, and even the rubber hoses on vehicles.

Porcupines (like moose) are attracted by leaves of the yellow pond-lily, which are unusually high in sodium. As they pursue the crucial mineral, you may see them nibbling pond-lily leaves along the borders of waterways, or swimming, buoyed by their quills, to reach the plants. They may also chew at sandy, mineral-rich soil along river banks or roadsides.

In our own back yards, some of us have suffered the effects of porcupines feeding on trees and shrubs. The animals also can have potentially far-reaching effects on the forest. For example, according to Gustavus naturalist Greg Streveler, who has conducted several environmental impact studies around Juneau:

> Porcupines in the Juneau area from Thane to Salmon Creek are undergoing a major irruption. . . . A considerable portion of hemlock trees are chewed at the butt.

> We estimate that more chewing has occurred during the last five to ten years than during the entire previous century.... Numerous trees, including many ancient ones, are extensively debarked at the base. A likely result will be basal rot and consequently greatly increased wind-throw susceptibility in future decades.

What changes may occur over time are not clear, but we do know that our prickly neighbors are an integral part of the forests and the natural processes that surround us. ●

(Left) Porcupines often visit human habitations in search of salt.

(Below) Evidence of porcupine chewing on the base of a hemlock tree along a trail in Juneau. The dark areas without bark, below and to the right in the photo, are evidence of old chewings. The large light patch at the center would have been made recently. Note the grooves made by the porcupine's incisors.

Keen
Critter

in Southeast

What's that tiny, bright-eyed creature with big ears and a long tail? "Keen's deer mouse" is the official name of the small rodents that until 1993 were thought to represent several different species and subspecies of deer mice in Southeast.

You've perhaps found the droppings of these creatures in a cabin or tent site, and you may have encountered them if you camped in an old cabin and woke to find something skittering over your sleeping bag, or – *arghh!* – running across your face. The critters are called "deer mice" because the coloring of their fur closely resembles that of deer such as our Sitka black-tailed. They are predominantly gray or grayish-brown, with white undersides and white feet. Even their long skinny tails are brown or gray on top and white underneath.

Deer mice are the most widespread and numerous small mammals in Southeast Alaska, but we seldom see them because they are active only at night. If we look carefully, though, we can often see evidence of their existence—small black droppings about the size of rice grains, pinched and twisted at one end; tiny tracks with toe-prints in the snow; chew marks on forest mushrooms or shed antlers; or balls of grass, paper, or mattress shreddings the animals use as nests.

Here a mouse, there a mouse

Deer mice are very prolific, and their numbers can increase quickly. Females can begin breeding in their first year, and each male may breed with several females. A female typically has four to five young in a litter, but may have as many as 10 or 11. Young mice grow quickly. They are weaned in three or four weeks and can probably live on their own once they're about a month old.

People who study small mammals in Southeast Alaska have long observed that deer mouse populations fluctuate substantially from year to year. Populations seem to peak every five or six years, then drop, then peak again in a kind of cycle.

Researchers Thomas Hanley and Jeffrey Barnard of the U.S. Forest Service Pacific Northwest Regional Laboratory in Juneau noted that food availability is a major factor in deer mouse population levels, since it influences female aggression, social tolerance and dispersion, and survival, growth, and maturation of juvenile mice.

Their research on Chichagof Island showed that in 1993, for example, there was an abundant berry crop, and the breeding

Deer mice have long, skinny tails, and the coloring of their fur resembles that of Sitka black-tailed deer.

season lasted longer into the autumn than usual because of low population density (and low aggression in adult females). A highly productive spruce-seed crop that winter favored overwinter survival, and there was a major increase in mouse populations across a variety of habitats.

Though deer mice eat a variety of foods, they prefer fruits and seeds, whose abundance may vary substantially from year to year. Hanley and Barnard found mice on Chichagof Island ate mostly the fruits and seeds of understory plants (69 percent of overall stomach contents).

Southeast deer mice eat primarily fruits and seeds. They are important food for martens and owls.

The mice they studied preferred the fruits and seeds of salmonberry and stink currant. They also ate tree seeds and leaf material, but mice apparently do not digest the fibrous leaves and stems of plants well. Among tree seeds they preferred Sitka spruce, which are believed to be especially important in winter and early spring. The mice also ate blueberries, beetles, devil's club and elderberry seeds, and small amounts of fungi.

What good is a mouse?

If deer mice are so prolific, why isn't Southeast completely overrun with them?

Partly because as tidy packages of protein with few defenses except running away, deer mice are ideal prey for larger carnivorous animals. They are, in fact, a kind of "renewable resource." Since they are active primarily at night, their main predators are animals that hunt by night—owls, martens, and weasels.

In studying martens over several years on Chichagof Island, Alaska Department of Fish and Game researchers Rod Flynn and Tom Schumacher found that martens survived primarily by eating small mammals. "We found that martens prefer voles," Schumacher said, "but they eat mice because mice are more numerous than voles."

Deer mice and other small mammals are also an important food of most owls. In one study of some 400 owl pellets, about 80 percent of the contents were of deer mice; the other 20 percent were of voles and shrews. Another study showed that deer mice comprise up to 80 percent of the diet of northern saw-whet owls. And when the major food groups of owls are summarized in *Biology and Natural History of North American Owls,* small mammals make up more than 90 percent of the diet of most species of owls that occur in Southeast Alaska.

Mice may be particularly important prey in another sense. Since they are active all winter, even above the surface of the snow, they may be especially important for owls and other predators at a time of year when not many food resources are available.

Mice may also play another important role in Southeast forests. Although they do not eat large quantities of fungi, they may, like the flying squirrels we described elsewhere in this book help disperse the spores of truffles, the below-ground fruiting bodies of fungi that depend on small mammals to spread them around in the forest. (See "Nuts About Truffles," also in the Mammals section of this book.)

Deer mice undoubtedly eat a great many seeds that might otherwise germinate into plants, particularly Sitka spruce. But mice drop seeds when they are feeding, perhaps moving them to places with more potential for future germination and growth. If their seed caches are forgotten or for other reasons never retrieved, the seeds within them may sprout on favorable ground. Mouse droppings also provide fertilizer to help young seeds and plants grow.

Mice may also have less beneficial effects on ecosystems. Juneau naturalist Mary Willson has suggested that mice may eat songbird eggs; and in one case they were found to be major predators on seabird eggs on Triangle Island, British Columbia. Researchers Louise Blight, John Ryder, and Douglas Bertram reported that "mouse depredation was likely responsible for the loss of more (*rhinoceros auklet*) eggs than all other causes combined, with mice commonly opening and eating eggs of nearly twice their mass. In one study plot, mice depredated up to 34% of eggs."

The researchers noted that predation on the seabird eggs may increase in years of low marine productivity, when adult birds must increase their foraging time and leave the eggs unprotected. As Alaskans wrestle with questions of whether our fish, especially small "forage" species, are being depleted faster than they are being replaced, the interactions of deer mice and seabirds offer one small example of how events far at sea can influence even what happens miles away on land.

Getting out and about

Deer mice have a number of physical features that seem especially useful for their nocturnal existence. They have large eyes with night vision; large ears, indicating a strong dependence on hearing; long whiskers they can use to feel their way around in the dark; and a keen sense of smell.

In winter, besides huddling together to conserve heat, they can drop into brief states of torpor, slowing their body functions to conserve energy in the cold.

Deer mice also have very strong navigational instincts. In one study, a number of adult mice returned "regularly and swiftly" to a house after being released nearly three-quarters of a mile away. In another, one mouse that was displaced returned home from two miles away, and six of them returned from more than a mile away.

Deer mice are most active during the hours of darkness. Several adaptations, such as large eyes for night vision and long whiskers to help feel their way around, increase their ability to function at that time.

Deer Mice and Hantavirus

In the continental United States and Canada, deer mice have become unwelcome in homes and buildings because they've been identified as the carriers of several strains of *hantavirus*, which causes respiratory illness in humans. Hantavirus was identified in 1993 in the southwestern United States, but it has probably been affecting humans for centuries. The disease is very rare, but nearly 40 percent of the people who contract it have died, so it is an ongoing concern of both U.S. and Canadian public health agencies.

Hantavirus is carried in the droppings, urine, and mucous of deer mice that have been infected, and it can be transmitted when virus particles are dispersed in the air, as, for example, when people create dust by sweeping out little-used buildings where mice have been living, and don't let the dust clear before they move in.

In March 2004, the U.S. Centers for Disease Control (CDC) reported there have been 363 cases of hantavirus in 31 states, particularly California, Arizona, New Mexico, and Washington; more than a third have been fatal. Canada had reported 33 cases as of May 2000; 13 of those victims died.

Six of the cases reported in Canada were in British Columbia, but according to the CDC web site, as of March 2004 no cases of hantavirus have been reported in Alaska, and tests of deer mice in Alaska have failed to turn up any sign of the virus.

We found the CDC web site had excellent suggestions for avoiding exposure to hantavirus if you travel to areas where the virus is found.

Bob's Recollections

Raven, the Mice, and the Weasel

One winter we had an unusually large number of deer mice invade our home. We didn't want to kill them, so were live-trapping them; but decreasing their numbers was a slow process.

One evening a white weasel showed up in the kitchen, and the mice started disappearing very rapidly. The weasel lived with us for about a week, and we were very happy to have her there.

Late one night, however, I woke with a start to the sound of Raven, my pet red-lored Amazon parrot, screaming loudly from his cage. I ran out to find him clinging to the inside top of the cage, with a small pile of feathers at the bottom and a very musty odor permeating the area.

I knew what had happened. Our friendly weasel had run out of mice and was looking for other food.

So for a few nights Raven slept in the bedroom with us while I tried to live-trap the weasel. I finally attracted her with meatballs. We displaced her many miles away in the forest, where she belonged. I did notice when we released her that a small chunk was missing out of one ear. I could only think that Raven had had at least some small success in defending himself from the best mousetrap we ever had.●

NUTS about TRUFFLES

What good are squirrels?

Most of us encounter red squirrels when they have ripped out armloads of insulation from our cabins, or gnawed holes to get into our attics, or made off with disgraceful quantities of the food we've put out to attract birds. Fewer of us have seen Southeast's northern flying squirrels, which feed primarily at night and are seldom active during the day.

Both species of squirrels occur naturally on the Southeast Alaska mainland and on many of the islands south of Frederick Sound. Red squirrels were introduced on Baranof and Chichagof Islands in the mistaken belief they would provide food for martens introduced there in the 1930s and '50s. The red squirrels now found on Ad-

miralty Island were also recently introduced. Only flying squirrels are found on Prince of Wales Island.

Though they sometimes damage trees and prey on nestling birds or eggs, squirrels —and especially flying squirrels—play an important role in Southeast Alaska forests. They help disperse the spores of specialized fungi that promote the health and well-being of trees and other plants in the forest.

We see the fruiting bodies of *ectomycorrhizal* fungi when they sprout aboveground as mushrooms. But hidden below ground are extensive networks of fine white threads called *hyphae* that the fungi send out through the soil in all directions.

When hyphae come in contact with a soft young tree root, they wrap themselves

With membranes that stretch between their front and back legs, northern flying squirrels glide through the forest as if they had wings.

145

around it, forming a kind of sheath that encases the root tip. They penetrate into the root, grow in the spaces among the root's cells, and become essentially inseparable from the root itself.

As they grow and spread out, hyphae tremendously expand the ability of roots to absorb minerals, nitrogen, and water to feed the tree. They produce growth-regulating chemicals that induce the tree to produce new root tips, and they displace or fend off other fungi, bacteria, and nematodes otherwise poised to attack vulnerable roots.

In return, the host tree supplies food in the form of sugars, which the fungi cannot produce on their own because they do not possess chlorophyll for conducting photosynthesis. It's a classic symbiotic relationship from which both the trees and the fungi benefit.

Some ectomycorrhizal fungi are truffles that grow entirely underground, forming fruiting bodies that look like small potatoes. Unlike fungi that fruit above ground and scatter their spores on the wind, truffles cannot reproduce unless animals such as squirrels, mice, or voles dig them up and eat them. When a flying squirrel eats a truffle, the spores pass into the squirrel's digestive system, where they mix with yeast and nitrogen-fixing bacteria. This blend then ferments and is eventually compacted into pellets that the squirrel excretes.

The spores of the truffle, encased in pellets, are thus spread throughout the forest, where they germinate into fungi that help the forest trees to thrive.

Truffles work hard to be sure they will be eaten. When they are mature they emit strong odors. Smelling like fruit, fish, cheese, or garlic, they lure hungry squirrels to dig into the ground after them—savory meals with ulterior motives of their own. ●

Plants

Broad-petalled Gentian

Plants in Southeast Alaska

Fireweed

Plants are abundant in Southeast Alaska. Within the region we have the world's largest temperate rainforest—the Tongass. According to the U.S. Forest Service this forest may contain the highest biomass (concentration of living organisms per square foot) on earth. While tropical rainforests may have more species of plants, the Tongass is estimated to have five to eight times their biomass.

The number of plant species in Southeast is also impressive for our latitude. We have more than 900 species of vascular plants (ferns and their allies, conifers, and flowering plants). Add to this several hundred species of nonvascular plants, especially mosses, and the list is indeed impressive. Except for steep cliffs and glaciers, most of the region is vegetated.

With so many plant species surrounding us, each with a fascinating story, it was difficult for us to choose which ones to write about. However, we found a few that especially caught our interest.

We always look forward to seeing the first flowers of spring. A few plants bloom many weeks before most others, and we wondered why. Why bloom when there is still a danger of frost? What is around to help pollinate these plants so early in the year? Our curiosity led us to write the article on "The First Spring Flowers."

Salmonberry

If you are going to talk about plants in Southeast you must cover Sitka spruce. It's a prominent tree in the coastal rainforest and one that many animals we enjoy seeing depend upon. It's also the official Alaska State Tree, so we researched and wrote "Ouch! It's the Alaska State Tree."

Another important Southeast plant is the Nootka lupine. One of its roles is to help prepare our recently deglaciated areas and coastal meadows for the eventual establishment of the coastal rainforest.

What really got us interested in lupines, though, was how lupines use color to signal their main pollinator, the bumblebee. We wrote about this and other intriguing aspects of lupines in "Not Just Another Pretty Face."

We have always been intrigued by plants that eat insects, of which Southeast has at least four species. Learning about these led to looking at other plants that do not depend entirely on photosynthesis for food. All of these plants are either "odd-looking" or "odd-acting" in comparison with most plants. We put them all together in the article on "Oddball Plants."

Arctic Daisy

Plants in the orchid family are amazingly common in Southeast, but most species are small or do not have showy, spectacular blossoms. The mechanisms orchids have developed for survival and pollination are quite unique among plants of this region, so we wrote about them in "Wild Orchids."

On one September hike into the alpine we noticed many plants had turned brilliant red, while others were intense yellow or orange. We wondered if this unusual intensity of color could be found in other places, so we contacted Rich Gordon, who took Bob to some prime sites where he has found fall colors over the years. What they saw led to the photo essay "Fall Colors in Southeast Alaska."

Our favorite book covering Southeast plants is *Plants of the Pacific Northwest Coast* edited by Jim Pojar and Andy MacKinnon. We like this book for its excellent color photos and detailed plant descriptions. We also recommend *Native Plants of Southeast Alaska* by Judy Hall. That book uses the plant keys from *Anderson's Flora of Alaska* by Stanley Welsh, which contains the best keys for identifying Southeast plants that we have found.

The First Spring Flowers

The blooming of early blueberries in Southeast coincides with the arrival of rufous hummingbirds and the emergence of queen bumblebees.

(Preceding page) Rufous hummingbird approaching an early blueberry in blossom.

Purple mountain saxifrage often blooms in mid-April as soon as the snow has melted. It usually grows on rocky outcroppings near glaciers and in the alpine.

Why would a flower bloom in April

in Southeast Alaska, when there's still a chance of snow and cold weather? The reasons might be related to pollination, the transfer of pollen (containing male sex cells) from the male part of a flower to the female part, or from male to female flowers. Pollination is necessary to produce seeds, one of the ways in which plants reproduce.

We can think of a number of ways that being first out of the starting gate would help plants with pollination. Perhaps competition for insects or birds to help with pollination is lower early in the season, or perhaps a special pollinator is around then. Perhaps it's easier for a flower to be seen when other plants around it are not yet blooming. Perhaps flowering early in the spring allows more time and energy for growing during the rest of the summer.

Early blueberries (*Vaccinium ovalifolium*) grow as shrubs usually three to five feet tall. Found widely throughout Southeast forests, forest openings, and bogs, they often grow intermingled with Alaska blueberries (*Vaccinium alaskaense*), which bloom later and which many Alaskans call black huckleberry.

The blossoms of early blueberries generally appear before the leaves on the bush have developed, so they stand out in the forest like thousands of tiny, pink Japanese lanterns. They are one of the only flowers available for the nectar-sipping rufous hummingbirds that return to Southeast each spring after wintering in Mexico. Blueberries also may be pollinated by early emerging queen bumblebees.

Early bumblebees are probably important to another early blossoming flower in Southeast: **purple mountain saxifrage** (*Saxifrage oppositifolia*). Saxifrage flowers may be seen less frequently than others because they tend to bloom on rocky outcroppings that may be surrounded by snow and not easy to reach until after the flowers are gone. Near sea level purple mountain saxifrage are often found close to glaciers, on places such as the exposed rock at the face of Mendenhall Glacier in Juneau.

The flowers of purple mountain saxifrage are probably pollinated by queen bumblebees, which overwinter by hibernating in the frozen soil. The bees emerge about the same time the saxifrage blossoms open and are believed to be especially attracted to the purple flowers. Feeding on both pollen and nectar, the bees gather particles of pollen on their hairy bodies and carry them from flower to flower.

The bright yellow flags of **skunk cabbage** (*Lysichitum americanum*) often emerge even before the snow is gone in damp, marshy places throughout South-

east Alaska. Enclosed within a protective sheath, hundreds of tiny flowers cluster on a candle-shaped stalk, or *spadix*. The flowers attract hundreds of tiny beetles (*Pelecomalius testaceum*) that come to feed on the pollen the flowers produce and end up carrying pollen particles from flower to flower and plant to plant.

Our friend Mary Willson, an ecologist in Juneau, said skunk cabbage plants probably come up in spring as soon as the water in the ground around them is slightly above freezing. She said early blooming probably helps assure that beetle pollinators will find skunk cabbage plants before they are hidden by the growth of other forest vegetation.

What helps pollinate the delicate blossoms of the **fern-leaved goldthread** (*Coptis asplenifolia*)? The diminutive goldthread grows in deep forests throughout Southeast, often amid moss. Its leaves stay green all year long, and in winter it provides important forage for deer. In spring, its delicate, hardly-noticeable flowers burst like tiny comets trailing miniscule streams of light against the forest floor.

We were curious about what pollinates these tiny, early-blooming flowers. Upon close examination we saw tiny flies and

The fern-leaved goldthread appears to be pollinated by tiny flies and small beetles.

beetles crawling on them eating both pollen and nectar.

According to Willson the most common of these pollinators are dance flies. ●

Skunk cabbage often grows in large patches in Southeast. Deer eat the emerging blossoms and leaves, and bears eat the stems below ground level in the fall.

Ouch! It's the Alaska State Tree

Rich evergreen forests drape the mountainsides of Southeast Alaska and soothe the glacier-scoured landscape with a thick cloak of green. Residents and visitors alike grow hushed and quiet beneath the sifted green light of canopies sometimes hundreds of years old.

Some of the largest and most prominent trees in those forests are Sitka spruce, the species named the Alaska State Tree in 1962.

Sitka spruce are easily distinguished from the other large conifers that help make up the forest tapestry. While the needles of western hemlock, mountain hemlock, and red or yellow cedar have soft, rounded ends, Sitka spruce needles end in hard, sharp points. Wonder if a tree is a spruce? Just touch a branch, and if it bites you back, you'll know it's the Alaska State Tree.

Sitka spruce are one of 40 species of spruce found in North America, but they are the only truly coastal species. They grow only where there is no summer drought, and where maritime influences virtually guarantee fog, high humidity, and plenty of moisture.

Southeast Alaska's climate must be virtually ideal for them. Here they may grow 150 to 250 feet high—taller than a seven- to 10-story building. Their trunks may be five to eight feet in diameter, and some grow even larger.

What's surprising is that the root systems supporting big trees like these are often startlingly shallow, as you can see when you come across big spruce trees blown over in the forest. Sitka spruce roots may grow more than five feet a year, but most of that growth is lateral. In Southeast soil they may grow down a mere six inches before they're stopped by saturated soil.

Partnerships

To help in gathering nutrients (their other main function besides anchoring the tree), spruce roots form mutually beneficial relationships with certain fungi in the soil. These *mycorrhizal fungi* have extensive networks of fine threads called *hyphae* (HY-fee), which spread throughout the soil. The fine threads wrap themselves around young tree roots and expand the ability of the roots to absorb minerals, nitrogen, and water to feed the tree. In return, the host tree supplies them with sugars, which they cannot produce on their own because they do not have chlorophyll for conducting photosynthesis.

Large older spruce and other conifers also form partnerships aboveground. Their upper branches often provide prime conditions for the growth of lichens that can convert atmospheric nitrogen into a form that plants can use. When nitrogen leaches out of the lichens, or they die and fall to the forest floor, the nutrients within them become accessible to the host tree and to plants in the surrounding area. According to some studies, lichens may contribute as much as 50 percent of the nitrogen available to trees and other plants in certain forest settings.

Reproduction and growth

Al Harris, who served for many years at the Forestry Sciences Laboratory in Juneau, wrote in a paper we found on the internet about how Sitka spruce trees reproduce. He said that, beginning at about 20 to 40 years of age, spruce produce both male and

(Preceding page, top) Sitka spruce needles are distinctively sharp-tipped.

(Preceding page, bottom) One of the largest Sitka spruce trees accessible by trail is found along the Ward Lake Trail near Ketchikan. This forest giant is 215 feet high and more than six feet in diameter (measured at 10 feet above its base). The spruce and its neighboring trees are part of a Landmark Tree Site called Ward South Landmark Acre. Many trees in the site are estimated to be more than 300 years old.

(Left) Sitka spruce roots are surprisingly shallow, making the trees susceptible to windthrow, the primary means of forest regeneration in Southeast Alaska. The root wad Willette Janes is admiring here is on Peterson Creek Trail in North Douglas, near Juneau.

female cones. The reddish male cones grow on secondary branches lower down in the trees. The light-green female cones grow at the ends of primary branches near the tree's top. Male cones release pollen in spring (late April to early June), and it fertilizes the female cones, which ripen and produce seeds later that same summer.

Often prompted by dry weather, the cones usually begin releasing their seeds in October, then reclose during wet weather. Apparently most spruce seeds are released within six weeks, but others remain and are released throughout the following year.

One of the prettiest sights in Southeast forests is a large, fallen "nurse log" covered with moss and a long row of spruce and hemlock seedlings. The nurse log environment moderates the amount of water and encourages the growth of mycorrhizal fungi. As the log decays, it also gradually releases nutrients to nourish the young trees—and so an older generation of large trees paves the way for the growth of succeeding generations.

Sitka spruce grow especially well in three particular settings in Southeast, and that's where some of our largest trees are found. On deposits of soil and gravel where rivers have flooded, or at the mouths or junctions of streams, soil is usually well drained and it contains extra nutrients. Here conditions are close enough to ideal that spruce often achieve or almost achieve their full growth potential.

Spruce also grow well in areas underlain by *karst,* heavily eroded limestone and marble bedrock. On karst, acidic water from peatlands breaks down the minerals in limestone and marble, making them accessible to growing trees and plants. Underlying caves and fissures provide good drainage. And rocky crevices allow tree roots to take hold and anchor themselves against wind that might knock them down before they reach their full potential.

Spruce also grow especially well along streams where salmon spawn. Studies are

Female Sitka spruce cones are usually found in the top quarter of the tree.

Sitka spruce crops vary, Harris said, with good crops occurring at five- to eight-year intervals in Alaska.

In Southeast Alaska soils are so poor and there is so much competition from brush, many spruce seeds may not find suitable places to grow. If there's too much water close to the surface, delicate roots can suffocate. If there's too little water, the roots might dry out and wither. In some areas, rotten wood offers the only suitable seed bed.

now documenting how salmon carcasses act as fertilizer and provide nutrients such as nitrogen and phosphorus that benefit trees and other plants. One study, in fact, found that salmon carcasses produced 18 percent of the nitrogen in streamside trees.

What good is a spruce?

Sitka spruce wood is straight-grained and strong for its weight. It has traditionally been used for lumber, oars, planking, masts, turbine blades, and experimental aircraft. Tight, straight-grained spruce wood is remarkably resonant, and is prime stock for making guitar faces and the sounding boards of high quality pianos.

Native people have long used spruce roots, which grow long and have few branchings, in making baskets; and a number of organizations are exploring new possibilities for creating value-added products that will generate jobs and income from spruce and other forest resources.

One group of Southeast residents has also been locating and measuring some of Southeast's biggest Sitka spruce as part of the Landmark Trees Project. On the first 68 one-acre sites mapped in the Tongass National Forest, which encompasses most of Southeast's forests, members of the project have found Sitka spruce trees well over 200 feet tall, six to eleven feet in diameter, and more than 300 years old. The oldest probably reach 1,000 years.

Larger and older Sitka spruce seem to be of the greatest value to wildlife in Southeast. Brown bears make winter dens in root cavities of large trees at high elevations. All but one of 14 wolf dens located in one study on Prince of Wales Island were in cavities beneath the roots of large trees (not all spruce).

River otter and mink commonly den in stream banks stabilized by the roots of large

trees. And during severe winters Sitka black-tail deer congregate where tall Sitka spruce and western hemlock with broad canopies intercept the snow and make browse more accessible than in open areas.

Among birds, marbled murrelets nest in Sitka spruce, where sturdy upper branches, perhaps covered with moss, provide platforms for nesting and takeoff. And nearly 80 percent of 3,850 bald eagle nest trees examined in Southeast were in Sitka spruce. The trees were generally taller than those around them and had strong tops and branches.

Add to these uses the simple beauty of majestic columnar trunks and the delicate brush of rain sifted through a billion needles, and it seems the choice of our state tree was a happy one indeed.

In Southeast Alaska martens raise their young in snags, fallen trees, and cavities beneath the roots of large old trees such as Sitka spruce.

*Red crossbill,
female*

*Red squirrels
harvest spruce seeds
by picking ripe
female cones and
stripping them of
their scales as if
they were nibbling
and twirling an ear
of corn.*

*Red crossbills have
beaks that crisscross
at the tip, a design
especially effective for
removing seeds from
cones. The bird to
the right, with
red plumage, is
a male. This
particular male's
beak has a
lefthanded cross,
as opposed to the
female's in the
photo at the top
of the page, which is
righthanded.*

Seed Shuckers

Seeds and cones are surely important to spruce trees, but they're important to a number of forest animals as well. Red squirrels and some groups of both red and white-winged crossbills depend on spruce seeds for survival.

A single red squirrel may harvest as many as 12,000 to 16,000 spruce cones a year. Some they use at once, but they also cache great quantities of unopened cones to serve as food during the winter.

It takes a lot of spruce seeds to make a meal. The tiny reproductive packets are about as large as the head of a pin, and it takes about 210,000 of them to make a pound. They are tucked inside an inedible armor of hard, overlapping scales.

Yet it takes a squirrel only minutes to extract all the seeds from a cone. Holding the cone in its forepaws the small rodent will twirl the cone, flinging discarded scales in all directions, until only the bare rod-like core is left. Then it will move onto the next. Squirrels leave mounds of cores and cone-scales in the forest, often around the trunks of particularly prolific spruce trees. These *middens* can be huge—15 to 18 feet in diameter and sometimes three feet deep—and may serve as caches for winter supplies of unopened cones.

Crossbills—red (male) and olive-green (female) birds in the finch family—may be even more efficient at removing seeds. In contrast to most other songbirds, whose upper and lower beaks meet in a point, crossbills have upper and lower mandibles that curve in opposite directions and crisscross at the tip—a

design especially effective for removing seeds from cones.

First the birds use a lateral motion of the lower mandible to separate the overlapping scales of a cone and expose the seed. Next, they snake their long

tongue into the gap and pull out the seed. Finally, they use their beak and tongue to crack open the seed, discard its woody covering, and swallow the nutritious inner kernel.

This whole process takes only a few seconds, and feeding crossbills repeat it hundreds or thousands of times a day. Some studies say crossbills must shuck seeds nearly constantly to survive, and one study found a crossbill may ingest about 3,000 seeds a day. That's not bad work for a creature who must thwart the defenses of a tree determined to protect its seeds.●

Not Just Another Pretty Face

Lupines, the tall, purple spears of blossoms that brighten fields, roadsides, and alpine or subalpine areas in many parts of Southeast Alaska are not just beautiful flowers. If it were proper to talk of flowers in human terms, we might say they are remarkably clever, and in any terms they are among Southeast's hardiest pioneers.

Lupines thrive in nutrient-poor areas, so we find them growing in places newly uncovered by retreating glaciers, in disturbed areas, and sometimes where there seems to be little soil and mostly gravel. Lupines have a number of characteristics that help them survive where more fragile species may

not. Perhaps most importantly, they harbor nitrogen-fixing bacteria in nodules on their roots. These bacteria can pull nitrogen out of the air and incorporate it into organic compounds that nurture the lupines and enrich the soil for other plants that follow them.

Nitrogen is the nutrient most commonly deficient among the 14 that plants need. It is also the one used in greatest quantities by most plants. According to one estimate made in 1990, legumes (the plant family to which lupines belong) harvest 80 million tons of nitrogen a year from the air—more than the 50 to 60 million tons produced synthetically by fertilizer factories.

Lupines are hardy pioneers. They often grow in areas newly uncovered by retreating glaciers.

157

Lupines also have fine hairs, or "fur," on their stems and the undersides of their leaves. The hairs help deflect wind and some of the sun's radiant heat to keep the plants from drying out, yet they help hold in some heat to promote more favorable growing conditions.

Lupines anchor themselves in place by growing large, strong rhizomes—underground stems that extend both downward and laterally and that function much like roots. As many Southeast gardeners have discovered, individual lupine plants multiply by sending out horizontal extensions that root at intervals and emerge aboveground as separate, new plants. This allows the plants to reproduce without the tremendous output of energy required to flower and produce seeds. The plants produced by this method, however, are all clones with exactly the same genes and characteristics as the parent plants.

Fortunately for the hardiness of the species, as well as for those of us who enjoy their spectacular summer beauty, lupines also reproduce by flowering. This allows for cross-pollination, the exchange of genes among different plants, so that lupines as a species maintain genetic diversity and improve their chances of dealing with changing environmental conditions, both now and over the long term.

In Southeast Alaska lupines are cross-pollinated primarily by bees. Here's how it works:

Each of the blossoms clustered along the upright stem of a lupine has five unequal petals. The uppermost, called the "banner," stands upright, furled at the center, beckoning potential pollinators like a bright, showy flag. Two lateral petals called the "wings" fold together like cupped hands, enclosing two smaller petals that join together to form the curved, sharply pointed "keel." Inside the keel are the plant's reproductive organs, 10 hairlike stamens (the male pollen producers) surrounding a longer pistil (the female pollen receiver).

When a bee lands on a lupine blossom that is mature—ready to release pollen—the weight of the bee pushes the two wings apart, exposing the keel. The bee's weight pressing on the keel compacts the stamens and pistil inside it, pressing pollen out the keel's curved, pointed tip. The dust-like pollen is caught on the bee's hairy legs and underside.

At the same time the pistil, which stands up even higher than the stamens, is pushed out. It also brushes against the bee's underside, picking up pollen from other blossoms the bee has visited. Thus, the exchange of genes takes place among lupines visited in varying sequence by different bees, or by the same bees at different times. The bees, meanwhile, extract nectar from within the blossoms to feed the young within their own colonies.

What makes this whole exchange even more remarkable is that the lupines appear to have developed a means of signaling the bees so that pollen exchange is made with great efficiency. As with a number of other types of flowers, lupine blossoms shift color as they age—a signal the bees apparently can interpret so that they spend their energy visiting only blossoms that are at the right stage of maturity to release pollen (and, of greatest importance to the bees, nectar).

When lupines first begin blooming, the banners of individual blossoms have large

white patches. From a distance the total flower spear looks purple with white spots. As individual blossoms mature, the white spots darken, becoming all purple, or sometimes deep pink. The color shift progresses up the lupine stem as the blossoms mature, and in fact, on a single plant you can often see blossoms at the top that are still closed or just opening, blossoms toward the center

(Above) Bumblebees are important pollinators that respond to colour changes signalling the availability of pollen in lupine blossoms.

that are purple with large white patches on their banners, and blossoms toward the bottom that are all purple or purple and pink. In withered blossoms at the bottom of the stem you may be able to see green seed pods beginning to develop.

(Far left) Even this rare white lupine we found near Mendenhall Glacier has begun to turn purple. The more mature blossoms at the bottom of the stalk are no longer rich with pollen. Soon they will mature and produce seed pods like those shown in the photo to their right.

Barb Short, a botanist friend we met over the internet, told us she has seen similar color changes among bluebonnets, lupines of several species that are found in Texas. The process appears to be stimulated by pollination. "Once a flower is pollinated," she wrote to us, "the energy needs to be turned to seed production instead of making more nectar. . . . The color change warns the bee that there is no nectar available. If the bees visited all the flowers with no nectar, much of the pollen needed for unpollinated flowers would be lost." So using color signals saves energy for the bees and increases the efficiency of cross-pollination for the lupines.

Short said the chemical involved in the color change is proanthocyanin—a chemical similar to the one that colors beets, cherries, and violets.

Martha Weiss, a botanist from Washington, D.C., studied flowers, including lupines, and the bees that pollinate them. In a study of one lupine species, she found that bees visited blossoms that had not yet changed color 96 times, while during the same period bees visited blossoms that had changed color only 8 times. Weiss wrote in an article in *Nature* magazine:

> *It is often assumed that plants have a largely passive role in plant-animal relationships. . . . But I have shown that plants in at least 74 different families use colour changes to direct their pollinators to rewarding and sexually viable flowers. Through such signals, plants are able to play a surprisingly active part in their interactions with animals.*

Lupines may not interact directly with animals besides bees and other pollinators, but they do benefit birds such as sandpipers and arctic terns that nest in open locations by providing foliage that camouflages and shelters nests. And we have observed crab spiders using lupine blossoms as staging areas for capturing unwary insects.

According to Welch's *Flora of Alaska*, only one species of lupine—the Nootka lupine (*Lupinus nootkatensis*)—is widespread in Southeast Alaska. But several known varieties of Nootka lupine can take on different appearances, particularly in the size and density of the "fur" on their leaves and stems. These varieties also hybridize with the two other species that have a more limited distribution in Southeast, arctic lupine (*Lupinus arcticus*) and long-leaved lupine (*Lupinus polyphyllus*). ●

The white banners on the lupines below signal that they have nectar and are ready for pollination. Note the spotted sandpiper nesting at the base of the plant.

Wild
Orchids

A dance fly that probes into a green bog orchid blossom will likely emerge with clumps of pollen stuck to tiny disks on its head. The insect's subsequent visits to other flowers of the same species help promote the exchange of pollen between plants (cross-pollination).

(Preceding page)
Calypso bulbosa,
"fairy slipper"

(Right) White bog orchids may grow three feet high in Southeast Alaska, often rising above surrounding plants in a muskeg and emitting a strong, pleasant aroma similar to that of vanilla.

People the world over have long been fascinated with orchids. Wealthy collectors have paid fortunes to possess exotic varieties, and adventurers have risked their lives to extract rare varieties from jungles and remote locations.

In 2001, U.S. sales of potted orchids (artificially raised or hybrids) approached $100 million; and according to an item in *U.S. News and World Report,* a single potted white stem of a phalaenopsis orchid at the elegant Takashimaya Floral Boutique in New York was priced at $175. Nurseries and other outlets currently ship millions of orchids all over the United States and Canada, and their spectacular varieties and colors are often the highlight of garden shows and greenhouse displays.

Most people are attracted by the complex and elegant blossoms of orchids, and tropical species especially show a staggering variety of colors, petal shapes, and intricate markings.

A few wild orchids in Southeast Alaska have blossoms large and colorful enough to remind us of their more spectacular tropical relatives. Those are the beautiful *Calypso bulbosa,* or **"fairy slipper,"** found mostly on small islands of Southeast Alaska, often on the outer coast; and three species of **"lady's slippers"** occasionally found in the northern parts of our region.

But a number of other wild orchids are quite common in Southeast forests and bogs, and it's easy to discover and appreciate their lovely, delicate blossoms by just looking more closely or using a magnifying glass or hand lens.

Fairy slipper and lady's slipper blossoms display the quintessential orchid-type blossom. Each flower has several upright parts (petals and sepals), and a lower petal modified into a showy pouch that apparently serves as a landing pad for pollinating insects. Insects are attracted to the blossoms

by their color and fragrance, then when they probe the blossoms, they emerge carrying pollen that they subsequently deposit on other plants.

Some orchids go to great lengths to trick insects into helping with the process of pollination. They have developed blossoms that mimic both the appearance and the chemical sex signals, or pheromones, of female insects. The blossoms of *Chiloglottis tropeziformis,* an orchid not found in Southeast, looks and "smells" so much like a particular species of female wasp that males of the species are attracted to the orchid flowers from long distances. And the orchid *Coryanthes speciosa*, one of the species known as bucket orchids found in lowland forests in Central and South America, lures male euglossine bees into its heart, coating them with both pollen and a waxy perfume that appears to be useful in attracting female bees.

Here in Southeast Alaska, **white bog orchids,** which often grow in large patches in marshes and muskegs, emit a strong fragrance that some describe as a combination of vanilla, cloves, and other spices. They seem to attract certain insects, such as mosquitoes, dance flies, and moths, which help transport their pollen from one flower to another. The nectar in bog orchids is housed in a narrow pouch or "spur" that projects backward from the lip of the blossom, and it can only be reached by an insect with a long proboscis, or tubular mouth part. When the insect sticks its head into the blossom it bumps against and tears off tiny adhesive discs that stick to its forehead and proboscis, and pick up clusters of pollen that can then be deposited in another orchid blossom.

Heart-leaved twayblades—tiny orchids that are fairly common in moist or wet forests in our region—use a different approach. They give off a strong odor that attracts flies and fungus gnats. When they are touched by one of these insects, they shoot out a drop of viscous fluid filled with pollen grains. The fluid glues the pollen mass to the insect's body so it, too, can be carried to subsequent blossoms.

If pollination is successful, an orchid may produce for each blossom a single oval or oblong capsule filled with tiny seeds. A capsule may contain an enormous number of seeds—as many as 3,770,000 were counted in a single capsule of a tropical American orchid, *Cynoches chlorochilon,* for example. And it's a good thing, too. As A.F. Szczawinski writes in *The Orchids of British Columbia,* "Unless the conditions of temperature, moisture, soil and shelter are ideal, failure for the seedlings is certain. There is one chance in thousands that such ideal conditions will occur."

Once orchid seeds land on the ground, they do not germinate as easily as the seeds of most plants. Their outer seed-coat must be penetrated by the microscopic threads of certain fungi species in the soil before they can germinate. Apparently the fungi are needed to convert starches in the seed into simpler sugars that the embryo orchid can use.

Whether or not pollination is successful, it may be years before a particular orchid will bloom again. For this reason, as well

(Bottom) Rattlesnake plantain is named for the variable striations on its leaves, which often resmemble the markings of rattlesnake skin. Its blossom, shown above the photo of the leaves, displays delicate petals on a central spike.

Spotted coralroot is a saprophytic orchid that lives off decaying organic matter in the soil. Small clusters are often seen in the deep shade of coniferous forests in Southeast Alaska.

as their fragility and their dependence on associating with fungi growing in the soil around them, wild orchids in many parts of the U.S. and the world have become rare, and many states have laws prohibiting picking them.

Some orchids also reproduce by vegetative multiplication. This is true of the **rattlesnake plantain,** found in primary glacial forests and dense forests along the beach fringe in Southeast. This intriguing plant, with rosettes of mottled or striped evergreen leaves and delicate flowers on a slender spike, can spread very rapidly, "creeping" along under the ground by extending its underground stem, or rhizome.

In the case of the **bog adder's tongue** (*Malaxis paludosa*), found in bogs in Southeast Alaska, small projections known as "bulbils" grow at the tips of the leaves and break off to form new plants.

Two species of orchids seen fairly often in the deep shade of Southeast coniferous forests may not at first be recognized as orchids. Completely pink or yellowish and semi-transparent, the **coralroots** are saprophytic plants—they live off decaying organic matter and contain no chlorophyll for making their own food. Coralroot flowers nonetheless show orchid-like characteristics—their many-petaled blossoms have a characteristic protruding lip, though they are small and clustered along an upright spike.

Authoritative field guides list 21 species of wild orchids found in Southeast. To learn more about them we recommend *Native Plants of Southeast Alaska* by Judy Hall, and *Plants of the Pacific Northwest Coast* edited by Pojar and MacKinnon. ●

Elusive Promises

Calypso bulbosa, *"fairy slipper"*

Many people's inordinate fascination with orchids, or "orchidelerium," over the centuries probably stems from myths and traditions in a number of cultures. The Aztecs and Mayas of Middle America used vanilla, made from the seed capsules of orchids of the *Vanilla* genus, as an erotic drink; and once the Spanish carried vanilla flavoring to Europe in the 1700s, it was touted as a tincture or infusion to insure male potency. After Thomas Jefferson brought vanilla to the United States from France, it was enthusiastically accepted, and occasionally advertised to "stimulate the sexual propensities."

Women in Victorian England were forbidden to own orchids, whose name comes from the Latin *orchis,* meaning testicle and suggesting sexual associations. Even today the scent and flavor of vanilla is widely marketed for its sensuous and evocative qualities in soap and perfumes.

The "fairy slipper" *Calypso bulbosa* is named for the beautiful goddess who ensnared Homer's Ulysses for seven years on the island of Ogygia. The mountain lady-slipper, occasionally found in northern Southeast Alaska, is named *Cypripedium,* which means "the foot of Aphrodite," the ancient Greek goddess of love.

Oddball Plants

Throughout the world the great majority of plants have one fabulous ability in common—they can make their own food. Using energy from the sun (which is absorbed by chlorophyll, a green pigment in their leaves) they are able to combine water from the soil and carbon dioxide from the air to make glucose, a sugar that is carried throughout their structures to fuel their growth and the ability to reproduce.

But a few plants have diverged from this pattern. They get none or only a portion of what they need from the process called *photosynthesis*. They've found other ways to get the food they need, and one happy result is that they can live where more ordinary plants would have difficulty surviving.

We like to call these plants "oddballs," following the lead of Pojar and MacKinnon, editors of the excellent field guide *Plants of the Pacific Northwest Coast*.

A number of oddball plants are found in Southeast Alaska. On the following pages are portraits of five oddballs that we find most interesting.

Northern groundcone in bloom. Compare these plants with the one shown on the next page, photographed in early spring.

The aquatic bladderwort produces small "bladders" on its underwater roots. These act as tiny traps, capturing insects the plant then consumes.

Northern groundcone in spring

Northern groundcone

One of the oddest-looking plants you will see in Southeast is northern groundcone (*Boschniakia rossica*), a parasite that attaches itself to the roots of shrubby alders and feeds on their sap. It grows from a thick underground stem, and in spring it looks like a large pale pine cone standing upright on the ground.

The groundcone's tiny, overlapping "scales" are actually leaves. Tightly closed in the spring, they open later to reveal small, brownish-red flowers, each with a scale-like leaf beneath it.

Groundcone has no chlorophyll and makes none of its own food, so it always grows near its host plant. Look for it near alders throughout Southeast.

Pinesap

Another odd-looking character is pinesap (*Hypopitys monotropa*). This plant sends up stalks with fleshy pink or yellowish flowers. Pinesap contains no chlorophyll so it is not able to conduct photo-synthesis, but it can live in deep shade where plants that rely on photosynthesis could not survive. A member of the wintergreen family, it draws nutrients from dead and decaying vegetation in the soil.

Some studies indicate that pinesap may also tap into the underground network of mycorrhizal fungi associated with conifer trees such as spruce and hemlock. One study using radioactive carbon showed that filaments from mycorrhizal fungi, which wrap around and penetrate tree roots in conifer forests like ours in Southeast, can grow around the pinesap's root in the same way, forming a bridge and passing on nutrients that the fungi originally got from the tree.

Pinesap flowers are about half an inch long and form at the top of stalks up to about one foot tall. We have seen these plants only occasionally and have always found them in the darkest part of the forest.

Dwarf mistletoe

The dwarf mistletoe (*Arceuthobium tsugense*) is difficult to see because in our region it usually grows high up on western hemlock trees. But it's hard to miss the "witches' brooms" this parasite causes in infected trees. Dwarf mistletoe is in the same family as the variety you might stand under in hopes of getting a kiss. It contains some chlorophyll and can conduct photosynthesis to some extent, but it depends on its host tree for most of its food.

Starting as a tiny seed that lands on a tree branch or trunk, mistletoe taps into its host's sap by forming a holdfast with thin filaments that act very much like roots. These filaments, called *haustoria*, release special cellulose-dissolving enzymes that help them penetrate into the tree and divert water and dissolved nutrients from the tree into the mistletoe.

Branches on infected trees react to the mistletoe by growing abnormally. They become gnarly and deformed and often produce a profusion of sub-branches, forming obvious and recognizable "witches' brooms." In young trees the brooms may form into parallel stems so the tree looks as if it has several main tree trunks.

Dwarf mistletoe has a slow but effective reproductive process. About five years after a plant has infected a tree, it sends out leafless aerial shoots about three or four inches long. Each shoot produces tiny flowers that are either male or female.

Once fertilized, the female flower produces a small, berry-like fruit containing a single seed. It takes more than a year for this fruit to ripen, but once it does, a buildup and sudden release of hydraulic pressure in the shoot ejects the seed. The sticky seed may shoot as far as 50 feet away from the tree and travel at speeds up to 60 miles an hour.

Mistletoe seeds have been found in the feathers of several species of forest birds and also on the fur of red and flying squirrels. No doubt these animals help transport the seeds widely throughout the forest.

(Above left) Dwarf mistletoe female plant with berry-like fruit

(Above right) A witches' broom in a hemlock tree

Sundews

Many people in Southeast are familiar with round-leaved sundew (*Drosera rotundifolia*), the tiny insect-eating plant commonly found in muskegs and bogs. Long-leaved sundew (*Drosera anglica*) has the same carnivorous habits but has longer, narrower leaf blades that may be positioned to capture different types of insects.

Sundews are able to survive in wet, nutrient-poor soils because they capture and digest insects to supplement the food they make through photosynthesis. Their leaves are covered with long, reddish glandular hairs that exude drops of sticky fluid. When spiders or flying insects such as mosquitoes or gnats brush against the hairs, they are held fast, unable to escape. The glands respond by turning inward towards the center of the leaf, where enzymes are exuded to digest the nutritious prey.

We have found long-leaved sundews are particularly common around the edges of small muskeg ponds.

Common butterwort

Another carnivorous plant in Southeast is the common butterwort (*Pinguicula vulgaris*). It is sometimes called "bog violet" because its purple, white-throated blossoms resemble the flowers of violets. The butterwort's leaves, clustered in a rosette around the base of the plant, form a deadly trap for small insects. They are coated with a kind of mucilage, and insects that venture too close stick to their slimy upper surfaces as if they were caught on flypaper. The leaves also curl inward at the margins, making it even more difficult for a snared insect to escape.

Like sundews, butterworts secrete enzymes that digest the soft tissue of the insects. The plant uses this food to supplement what it can manufacture through photosynthesis.

We have seen butterworts in wet meadows and around the damp margins of ponds in newly deglaciated areas. ●

Fall Colors

in

Southeast

Alaska

(Preceding page)
Caltha-leaved avens
from a site overlooking
Douglas

What? Fall colors in a region where most of the trees are spruce and hemlock, and where most deciduous plants turn from green to brown with nothing in-between? Yes, you can find some spectacular colors in Southeast Alaska if you look in the right places. Here are some colors we found in the Juneau area one year in late September.

(Left) The Mendenhall Glacier area near the lake on September 17. Cottonwood and willow leaves provide most of the yellow.
(Below) Blueberry and willow

(Lower left) Blueberry and nagoonberry

(Above) Blueberry leaves

(Left) The subalpine just above the Mt. Roberts tram on September 19. Here the red colors are leaves of caltha-leaved avens and dwarf dogwood. The distant yellows on Mt. Juneau are leaves of deer cabbage.

(Below) Caltha-leaved avens and dwarf dogwood

Deer cabbage

Dwarf dogwood leaves in open areas tend to turn red and die whereas the plants under the forest canopy usually stay green all winter.

171

Gold Ridge on September 19. Most of the orange color is produced by sedges and dwarf willows. Note: Gold Ridge (passed on the way to Mt. Roberts) was named for the discovery of gold nearby, but we think the name could also apply to the fall colors it produces.

Interspersed with the sedges are patches of dwarf willow

 Thanks to Koren Bosworth for help identifying sedges, and to Rich Gordon for leading us to some beautiful color in the Mendenhall Valley.

A closer look at the sedges on Gold Ridge

Granite Creek basin on September 26. Most of the reds here were produced by the leaves of alpine blueberry.

The upper parts of Granite Creek basin were dotted with lovely patches of arctic sedge.

Fireweed

(Far right) Alpine blueberry

Where do fall colors come from?

The colors we see in leaves come from pigments produced by the leaves' cells. These pigments are *chlorophyll* that colors the leaves green; *carotenoids* that color the leaves yellow, orange and brown; and *anthocyanins* that produce shades of red.

In spring and summer, plants produce chlorophyll continuously as part of photosynthesis, or food production. In those seasons the green of chlorophyll overpowers colors from other pigments in leaves.

As fall approaches, chlorophyll production (and photosynthesis) slow down, and the yellows and oranges from carotenoids begin to show through. These colors have been in the leaves throughout the growing season, but not until fall are they "unmasked" by the loss of green. This is particularly noticeable in the brilliant yellow leaves of some cottonwood trees in Southeast Alaska.

The reds and purples we see in some leaves are mostly from anthocyanins, pigments that some plants produce in the fall.

Anthocyanins develop in the sap of leaf cells in late summer, forming when phosphates move out of the leaves, and sugars trapped in the sap break down in the presence of bright sunlight. The exact colors produced depend on the pH (or acid/base level) of sap and the amount of sugar trapped in the leaves. When the green from chlorophyll is depleted, reds appear, masking the yellow pigments that are also present in the leaves. We found reds most evident in the foliage of dwarf dogwood and caltha-leaved avens.

The yellow, gold, and orange in leaves remain fairly constant from year to year because the pigments causing them are always present. Weather does not affect the amount of carotenoids in leaves.

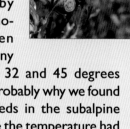

The brilliance of red pigments, however, can be affected by weather. More anthocyanin forms when the weather is sunny and cool (between 32 and 45 degrees Fahrenheit). This is probably why we found the most brilliant reds in the subalpine around Juneau where the temperature had been cooler than at lower elevations.

Contrary to popular belief, although frost may temporarily deepen the reds in some leaves, continued freezing temperatures usually stop the coloration process and cause leaves to shrivel and turn brown.●

Other Natural Things

Insect-Egg Mass Slime

Other Natural Things

Bob & burls

To conclude our explorations in this book, we have diverged from the preceding categories of living things to a few subjects that especially interested us.

You can hardly go anywhere in Southeast Alaska without coming across lichens. Many lichens are beautiful or unusual looking, and they contribute a great deal to the well-being of our forests and other habitats, and to the animals that live here. We learned a lot when we started "Lookin' at Lichens."

But what really got our attention were the unusual-looking and -acting slime molds. Once we learned how they creep about the forest, take on different shapes, and join together in huge conglomerations, we just had to write "Help— I've Been Slimed!"

Isopod

On a hike through a Southeast bog Bob came across a large fly standing on its head in the middle of a yellow avens blossom. Upon closer examination he discovered that a spider, exactly the same color as the flower, was holding and feeding on the fly. Our curiosity about these creatures led us into the fascinating world of crab spiders and the article "Charlotte Without a Web."

On occasion, Bob has helped prepare environmental analyses of particular areas in Southeast Alaska. To properly analyze potential environmental effects of a project, you need to pay special attention to species that are rare or especially sensitive. Besides the animals listed under the U.S. Endangered Species Act, a number of other animals and plants fall under state or other federal categories of concern. We have never found a single listing of endangered or threatened species, species of special concern, and sensitive species for Southeast Alaska. So we did a fair amount of research and cataloged the results in "Extinction: A Fate Worse Than Death."

Alaska is a place where harsh weather places a burden on a number of animals, including humans. Bob had researched and written an article about how to stay warm and dry in Southeast's wet and sometimes cold outdoors environment. That led us to write an article about hypothermia in humans, but in doing so, we discovered that many animals use hypothermia to survive inclement weather. That led to more research and the article "Chilling Out."

But then (Now see how this process works? Once you start asking questions you are hooked!) we discovered that some animals cope with Southeast winters by manufacturing a sort of antifreeze or actually freezing and coming back to life. We describe these incredible processes in "To Freeze or Not To Freeze."

One of our favorite places to be on a warm summer day is in the alpine. There's an amazing variety of flowers. Birds and mammals may be visible and fun to watch. And of course there are magnificent views. We describe and depict some of our favorite alpine flowers, birds, and mammals in "Life in the High Country."

Most of our favorite books on topics in this section are about how living things adapt to winter. They include *Life in the Cold* by Peter J. Marchand, *A Naturalist's Guide to the Arctic* by E.C. Pielou, and *Winter World* by Bernd Heinrich. We also especially enjoy the beautiful photos and text in *A is for Arctic* by Wayne Lynch.

Purple club fungi

Lookin' at Lichens

It may never compete with birdwatching, but looking at lichens can be a fascinating pastime—and a lifelong study if you get hooked on it. Southeast Alaska is a great place to see lichens. Lichenologists have counted some 500 species here, and they attribute these substantial numbers and species variety to clean air, a maritime climate with substantial moisture and moderate temperatures, and the presence of old-growth forests, which provide a variety of different habitats and further balance out light, moisture, and temperatures.

Many lichens are small. We see them snuggled against tree trunks or old exposed roots, or growing as faint patches of color on rocks and boulders. But some, like Methusela's beard or witch's hair, festoon our trees like Christmas icicles or "spider webs" hung up for Halloween. You'll find lichens along hiking trails, on glacial outwashes, or in amongst the moss in bogs. We found 25 different kinds, in fact, in just one of our backyards. And they can be seen all year round, except when they're covered with snow.

Lichens are neither plants nor fungi. They are partnerships between fungi and either algae or cyanobacteria (also called blue-green "algae") or both. Algae and cyanobacteria can conduct photosynthesis, but fungi cannot, so in lichens the fungi provide the "body" or form, while the algae or cyanobacteria produce enough carbohydrates to feed both partners.

Partly because they combine important characteristics of two different organisms, lichens can grow under more difficult conditions than almost any other living things. They live in deserts and

Some Cladonia *lichens form tiny "pixie cups" that help disperse particles for reproduction. This* Cladonia *is growing in a clump of moss on a fallen log.*

177

polar environments, withstanding extreme cold or heat. They live on mountaintops and barren rocks, absorbing water and dissolved minerals from rain and fog. During hard times they simply dry out and wait till conditions are favorable again.

They take on an amazing variety of interesting shapes and forms, and many have intriguing common names that reflect their unusual appearance. In Southeast we have lichens called forking bone, tattered rag, pincushion orange, devil's matchstick, frog pelt, pimpled kidney, and of course witch's hair and speckled horsehair.

Studies are finding that lichens serve a great many purposes in various settings. In Southeast Alaska they:

- help break down rocks to make soil;

- fix atmospheric nitrogen from the air and pass it on to trees and other plants (nitrogen is a vital nutrient and is often missing or very scarce in Southeast soils);

- provide nesting materials and camouflage for a number of birds, including thrushes, chickadees, hummingbirds, and warblers;

- during hard winters provide what may be the only available food for animals such as Sitka black-tailed deer, flying squirrels, deer mice, voles, and mountain goats; and

- serve as indicators of air quality because they readily absorb and concentrate contaminants such as sulfites, toxic metal compounds, and radioactive particles.

George Schenck, the author of *Moss Gardening,* even suggests ways to use lichens to add interesting colors and textures to gardens and landscaping—an idea that's a natural for many of us in Southeast.

We've explored some common Southeast lichens and their uses in the photos and captions below. If you'd like to know more about different types of lichens some good references are Pojar and MacKinnon's *Plants of the Pacific Northwest Coast,* which has a 20-page section on the most common lichens of our region; *Mosses, Lichens, and Ferns of Northwest North America* by Dale H. Vitt, Janet E. Marsh, and Robin B. Bovey; and the latest, most definitive word on lichens—the 800-page, color-illustrated *Lichens of North America* by Irwin M. Brodo, Sylvia Duran Sharnoff, and Stephen Sharnoff.

"Toy Soldier"

With its bright red fruits and abundant scale-like lobes, "toy soldier" (*Cladonia bellidiflora*) is one of the more easily identified small lichens in Southeast.

We usually see it amidst moss on the ground or on rotting wood.

Reindeer Lichen

Reindeer lichens, species of *Cladina* sometimes called "reindeer moss," form large mats in Southeast muskegs. Like *Usnea* lichens, they are a source of usnic acid, a mild antibiotic used in topical ointments. In other parts of Alaska they are a crucial source of carbohydrate energy for caribou in winter, when little other forage is available. Unfortunately they sometimes concentrate pollutants and pass them up the food chain to people.

Lungwort

This species of *Lobaria* belongs to a group called "lungworts" because of their resemblance to lung tissue.

Some species of *Lobaria* convert atmospheric nitrogen to forms that lichens and plants can use, and are considered good indicators of rich, unpolluted, often very old forests. In some studies *Lobaria* in old-growth forests contributed up to 50 percent of the total nitrogen output.

Lobaria lichens are comparatively high in protein. One study in Southeast found mountain goat feces in winter contained 18 to 30 percent lichen, mostly *Lobaria*. That suggests these arboreal lichens are an important survival food in times of scarcity.

Methusela's Beard

Methusela's beard (*Usnea longissima*) is common in Southeast Alaska spruce-hemlock forests. It can grow to nine feet long.

One of the most pollution sensitive lichens, *Usnea* is now nearly extinct in Europe, apparently because of widespread air pollution.

Usnea lichens look similar to *Alectoria* (witch's hair), but *Usnea* strands have a central cord that you can see if you pull one apart. *Alectoria* lichens do not.

Whiteworm Lichen

Whiteworm lichen (*Thamnolia vermicularis*) is common in the alpine in Southeast Alaska. It is unusual because it reproduces only by fragmentation. Pieces break off and are carried away, perhaps on the feet of birds or other animals, in the wind, or in avalanches.

Bull's Eye Lichens

Bull's eye lichens (species of *Placopsis*) are often the first plant-like organisms to become established in areas newly exposed by the retreat of glaciers. Their ability to help break down rocks and create soil, and to fix nitrogen from the air, helps pave the way for colonizing plants.

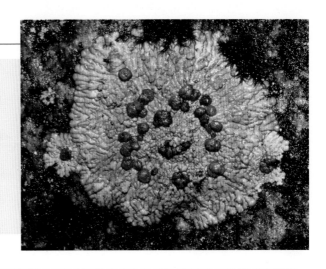

Crustose Lichens

These "crustlike" lichens are tightly attached to a rock in the alpine. Lichens can grow several millimeters, or hundredths of an inch, into granite, and one study reported lichens growing 16 millimeters (more than half an inch) into sandstone. Lichens help build up soil when they break down rock—both mechanically by growing between rock crystals or along cracks, and chemically by producing weak acids that eat away at rock.

Crustose lichens may grow only thousandths of an inch a year and may live for hundreds of years.

Witch's Hair, Horsehair Lichens

Witch's hair (light green *Alectoria sarmentosa*) and horsehair lichens (species of dark brown *Bryoria*) are important winter survival foods for deer. One study found fecal samples from Southeast deer in March contained as much as 43 percent lichen, and the presence of lichen correlated well with increasing snow depth.

Northern flying squirrels also eat *Bryoria*, especially in winter, and make their nests out of it.

Help—
I've Been Slimed!

Scrambled-egg slime is often quite large – up to eight inches across or more. We usually see it on the ground over vegetation, on rotting wood, or migrating onto live plants. This cushion-shaped sample, about one inch thick, is a single cell with thousands, millions, perhaps billions of nuclei.

Have you been seeing aliens in the woods lately? During a certain wet spring and summer some years ago, folks as far apart as Dallas, Texas; Long Island, New York; and Boston, Massachusetts thought they were. When they saw pulsating yellow blobs "crawling" across their lawns, they called police, fearing aliens from outer space, or at the least some sort of virulent mutant bacteria.

In several other parts of the United States, people have called veterinarians, thinking their dogs were sick after seeing—let's say it gently—unusual-looking "dog vomit" on their lawns. And in Juneau one spring a woman called the Coopera-

tive Extension Service for help identifying a strange gelatinous material on the pots of some seedlings she'd put out—and it was growing!

It turns out people's dogs were not sick at all, and the odd and unusual "aliens" were living things quite different from other live things. Scientists now classify them as life forms that are neither animals, plants, fungi, or bacteria. Instead they are called "slime molds," and they've been placed in a separate taxonomic kingdom called Protoctista.

Slime molds are quite common in Southeast Alaska, for they thrive in cool, damp environments. We usually see slimes during a single, particularly obvious stage of their life cycle, and their remarkable colors and shapes are sometimes visible only with a hand lens.

A number of them have common names that reflect the way they might look to someone with a sense of humor. For example, we found references to slimes called Japanese lantern slime, carnival candy slime, pretzel slime, wolf's milk slime, and yellow fuzz-cone slime. The names of slimes shown in the photos with this article turned out to be pretty colorful as well.

Most slime molds have a fascinating life cycle, for they take many different forms. They begin as tiny spores, cast out into the world by their parent structures.

Those that land on moist surfaces—wet vegetation or rotting logs, for example—develop into amoeba-like cells that creep about their habitat and feed on tiny particles such as bacteria, fungal spores, and decaying organic matter.

Those that land in water—in ponds, puddles, or seeps—develop into "swarm cells," which have tiny, whiplike appendages they use to propel themselves through the

water. They, too, feed on tiny particles and microorganisms.

If the environment changes, cells at this stage can take on each other's forms. For example, if its damp surroundings are flooded during a rainstorm, an amoeba-like cell can grow appendages and transform into a swarm cell in a matter of minutes. If its wet surroundings dry up, a swarm cell can absorb its appendages and become an amoeba-like cell. Such transformations might take place several times as a slime mold develops.

One of the more beautiful slime molds found in Southeast Alaska is **coral slime**. *The fruiting body looks like a tangle of tiny icicles or coral. It is very small (usually three-eighths of an inch long or less). We have seen it quite often, mostly on the undersides of rotten logs in wet or moist settings.*

Tapioca slime may be the slime mold we most notice on the ground in Southeast. One of our largest, it can be up to five-eighths of an inch thick and 12 inches in diameter. As it ages it may come to resemble cauliflower.

(Above left) **Insect-egg mass slime** *produces a cluster of shiny egg-like cases, each about one-sixteenth of an inch long. It's often seen on moss.*

(Above right) **Chocolate tube slime,** *another slime common in Southeast Alaska, is usually about three-fourths of an inch high. We've often seen it on the cut ends of logs along trails. Its resemblance to tiny, densely packed miniature pipe cleaners accounts for its alternate name, pipe-cleaner slime.*

Even beyond that, if conditions become too dry or otherwise unfavorable, slime molds can produce a hard covering within which they might lie dormant for years, ready to emerge when environmental conditions improve.

But that isn't all. At some point when they are prompted by environmental or chemical signals we don't yet fully understand, slime mold cells come together to reproduce. Some fuse into a single mass, one giant cell with millions or billions of nuclei, like the scrambled-egg slime in our photograph.

This "plasmodium," which is often what looks like some alien "blob" invading lawns or gardens, continues feeding and growing. Eventually it produces fruiting bodies, stalked structures like tiny balls or capsules on toothpicks, filled with spores. The spores are then released to form new organisms.

Slime molds are "out of sight, out of mind," for most of us, but they can be strikingly colorful and beautiful if we come across them when they're large enough to draw our attention. Some people have even kept them in jars as pets.

How slime molds change into their various forms, and what chemical or other signals they respond to, are of great interest to scientists. They could offer clues about how stem cells differentiate to take on different forms and functions.

Slime molds may seem like "aliens" or strange creatures, but the transformations they undergo may be similar to those we see as human embryos differentiate from single cells into bodies with complex and differentiated structures and organs. Understanding how slime molds grow and change may give us new insights into how humans and other living things develop from simple beginnings. ●

Charlotte

without a web

Crab spiders wait motionless on flowers, then use their long front legs to capture insects that land in search of nectar or pollen. This spider has captured a fly after taking on the color of a large-leaved avens in a muskeg.

(Preceding page) Male crab spiders, like the one on top of this yellow female, are many times smaller than females. They hardly eat as adults, except for nectar and an occasional insect.

What's a spider without a web?

In Southeast Alaska she might be a crab spider, a remarkable arachnid quite different from the web spider memorialized in the famous children's story by E. B. White.

Crab spiders don't spin webs. Instead the females hide out on flowers and capture unwary insects such as bees and flies that visit blossoms in search of nectar or pollen. Female crab spiders increase their chances of hunting success by changing color to match the yellows or whites of blossoms they are resting on. It's a matter of "All the better to eat you, my dear"—and all the better to keep from being eaten by birds or other predators higher up on the food chain.

We've seen some of these mistresses of disguise on a number of flowers in Southeast, including bunchberry, large-leaved avens, and bog laurel. We set out to learn more about them, and here is some of what we found.

While she's waiting for a meal, a crab spider sits almost motionless with her long front legs extended. When an insect lands on her flower and begins feeding, she reaches out and grasps it with her long legs, then bites it with two sharp fangs at the tip of her jaws. Her fangs not only deliver a venom that kills or paralyzes the insect. They also inject the insect with digestive juices that begin to dissolve its tissues. The spider extracts her meal as a liquid using her stomach's powerful pumping action. This rather unique method of feeding generally leaves the outer shell of the insect intact.

How many eggs a female crab spider will be able to produce in a summer depends on how many insects she can eat and how much weight she can gain. As much as possible, she will eat voraciously.

Meanwhile, male crab spiders—many times smaller than females—devote their three to four weeks of adulthood to looking for and mating with any females they can find. They typically sneak up on their vastly larger partners (for there's a real danger the nearsighted females will mistake them for prey). If the female is not ready to mate, the male will guard her from other males until she is receptive; then, once mating is done, he will move on in search of other receptive females.

Adult male crab spiders hardly eat at all. They live mostly on energy from food they captured before maturity. Finding and guarding females can take a lot of effort, though, and some recent studies have found that male crab spiders sometimes dip into flowers and drink nectar, which would provide considerable energy without the extended effort of capturing prey.

Simon Pollard and fellow researchers propose in the journal *Animal Behavior* that nectar may also provide male spiders with much-needed liquid. All spiders drink rainwater and dew to replace the body fluids they

lose through evaporation. But males lose water faster than females because of their relative size, and they do not gain liquids from consuming insects as females do.

Although crab spiders do not spin webs, they nonetheless make silk, that incredibly strong fibrous protein that spiders extrude from spinnerets on their abdomens. Like

many other spiders, crab spiders lay down "draglines" when they move. These lines, which may be fastened at intervals, may serve as safeholds or be used to retrace a spider's path. Apparently male spiders follow lines laid down by other spiders, and this may lead them to females. Once a male reaches a receptive female, he may trap her for mating by wrapping her loosely in silk.

Crab spiders use silk in two other ways: A female's eggs are laid in a sac of silk attached to a plant; the sac will serve as a nursery for the two to three weeks it takes for the eggs to hatch. Later on, like the offspring of the arachnid heroine in E.B. White's story, spiderlings that are ready to strike out in the world spin delicate "parachute lines" of silk and practice what is called "ballooning." Climbing onto a post or branch, an adventuresome youngster faces into the wind, then releases a strand of silk from the end of its abdomen. The silken strand billows out behind the spiderling until it has enough lift to pick the spiderling up, carrying the youngster wherever the wind may blow.

With devices and adaptations like these, who needs a web?

Crab spiders often kill and eat prey much larger than themselves. This spider has secured a bumblebee with silk and is feeding.

Laurie Lamm

Extinction

A Fate Worse Than Death

A humpback whale leaps from the surface of the water and crashes back down, showering spray toward awestruck watchers on a boat. A sea otter bobs in a lazy back float at the fringe of a kelp bed. A bald eagle glides from the top of a giant spruce tree while trolling fishermen watch to see if it will snatch a fish from the water.

Most Southeast residents consider all three of these animals intrinsic parts of life in our region. They are bright spots in our days, creatures to wonder at, marvels that attract visitors from all over the world. But any one of them might have disappeared from our air and waters. Any or all of them could have become extinct.

Alaskan humpback whale populations were nearly eliminated by commercial whaling in the 1800s and 1900s. Sea otters were nearly wiped out by Russian and American fur hunters in the 1700s and 1800s. More than 100,000 bald eagles were killed in Southeast alone under the bounty system during Territorial days.

According to the most recent figures, at least 110 species, subspecies, and varieties of plants and animals are known to have become extinct in the United States since 1620, when the Pilgrims landed on Plymouth Rock. Another 416 may be extinct; no one has been able to find them in recent years. Many and perhaps all of these animals and plants could be gone forever.

Since 1741, when the first Russian explorers arrived, three species of animals have become extinct in Alaska – the Steller's sea cow, a sea mammal that weighed more than 8,000 pounds, and two birds: the spectacled cormorant, and the Eskimo curlew.

As far as we know, no plant or animal species have become extinct in Southeast Alaska since humans settled here. Federal and state agencies are working to continue that record by studying, monitoring, and in some cases protecting species that may be at risk. Here is why some of our region's animals and plants are in danger—and what is being done to prevent them from earning the ignoble title of "extinct."

Endangered Species

Under the U.S. Endangered Species Act an endangered species is "any species in danger of extinction throughout all or a significant portion of its range." Alaska also has its own Endangered Species Act, which states, "a species or subspecies of fish or wildlife is endangered when its numbers have decreased to the point that its continued existence is threatened." The federal law applies to all plants and animals whereas the state law applies only to fish and wildlife species.

One animal listed as endangered under both state and federal laws is the **humpback whale.** Humpbacks and other whale populations were severely decimated in most parts of the world by commercial whaling during the 1800s and 1900s. As numbers of one species were depleted and it became difficult

to profit from hunting them, whalers turned their attention to other species. Thousands of whales were killed and processed in Southeast between 1800 and 1920, many at short-lived stations located at Killisnoo near present-day Angoon, Tyee at the southern tip of Admiralty Island, and Port Armstrong near the south end of Baranof Island.

Humpback whales—rich in oil and relatively slow swimmers—were easy targets. Prior to commercial whaling, an estimated 15,000 humpbacks fed in the North Pacific. By the time they began to receive protection from the International Whaling Commission, their numbers had dropped so low the whales were on the verge of extinction.

Today their numbers have increased to an estimated 6,000 to 8,000 in the North Pacific.

A report for the National Marine Fisheries Service by Jan Straley, affiliate assistant professor of biology at the University of Alaska Southeast in Sitka, and fellow researchers estimated a population of at least 961 humpback whales for Southeast in 2000. This estimate is higher than those of previous years, suggesting that the population of humpback whales in Southeast has increased.

The world population of **short-tailed albatrosses,** seabirds seen in waters offshore

(Previous page)
Humpback whales are listed as endangered under the U.S. and Alaska Endangered Species Acts.

Sea otters were overharvested between 1742 and 1910, but their populations began recovering after they received protection in 1911. The Southeast Alaska population was among several boosted by translocations meant to reestablish otters across their former range.

of Southeast Alaska, was nearly wiped out between 1889 and 1940. Feather hunters killed more than five million of the birds at their breeding ground on the Japanese island of Torishima. Only 30 to 50 birds escaped—juveniles that happened to be off at sea during the final massacre.

Today, the U.S. Fish and Wildlife Service estimates the entire world population of short-tailed albatrosses is about 1,000 birds. This revival is due mostly to prodigious efforts by Japanese ornithologist Hiroshi Hasegawa, who devoted himself for 12 years to rebuilding the breeding colony at Torishima Island.

The U.S. Fish and Wildlife Service Landowner Incentive Program also has recently

Steller sea lions in Southeast Alaska are listed as threatened under the U.S. Endangered Species Act.

provided funds to help Alaska longline fishermen develop and install seabird deterrent devices to keep the birds from diving on baited hooks and being killed.

Threatened Species

Under the U.S. Endangered Species Act a threatened species is "a species which is likely to become endangered within the foreseeable future throughout all or a significant portion of its range."

The **Steller sea lion** was originally listed as threatened in 1990 under the Endangered

Species Act because over a 30-year period its entire U.S. population had declined by about 64 percent.

In 1997 Steller sea lions in Alaska were split into two separate stocks for study and management purposes. Animals west of 144° W longitude, an area that includes the Gulf of Alaska, the Aleutian Islands and the Bering Sea, were designated the western stock. Animals east of 144° W longitude, including those in Southeast Alaska, were designated the eastern stock. The status of the western stock was changed to endangered because of continued declines; the eastern stock was kept as threatened.

Although the number of sea lions in the western population continues to decline, the National Marine Fisheries Service (NMFS) considers the prospects for recovery of the eastern population to be encouraging. According to NMFS counts in Southeast, the number of sea lions older than pups has increased from 6,400 in 1979 to 8,700 in 1998. The number of pups born at Hazy and Forrester Islands off the Southeast coast has been increasing, and in fact Forrester Island is now considered the largest sea lion rookery in Alaska.

A number of **salmon stocks** from the Pacific Northwest have been listed as threatened under the U.S. Endangered Species Act, and fish from a few of these stocks migrate to Southeast Alaska. For example, a series of dams constructed in the Snake River in the 1960s and 1970s caused the population of **fall chinook salmon** to plummet from a run of about 70,000 to about 500 fish. Some of these endangered fish range into our waters, where they may be taken incidentally in Southeast fisheries. This has resulted in the closure or curtailment of some fisheries in Southeast in an effort to protect these last remnants of a threatened stock.

State of Alaska Species of Special Concern

A Species of Special Concern is "any species or subspecies of fish or wildlife or population of mammal or bird native to Alaska that has entered a long-term decline in abundance or is vulnerable to a significant decline due to low numbers, restricted distribution, dependence on limited habitat resources, or sensitivity to environmental disturbance."

This list of species draws attention to the status and needs of vulnerable species before they become critical and require more extreme and costly management actions.

The **Queen Charlotte goshawk** is the unique subspecies of the northern goshawk that nests and lives year-round in the coastal rainforests of Southeast Alaska and British Columbia. There is limited information about the number of goshawks in Southeast, but because their numbers appear to be quite low, and because it appears the birds rely on old growth forest for nesting and feeding, the amount of old growth lost to timber harvest and other activities such as mining and urban development is considered a threat to their long-term survival.

The Alaska Department of Fish and Game and the U.S. Forest Service have been studying goshawks cooperatively since 1991. By studying goshawk movements, habitat use, home ranges, and nesting areas the agencies will understand how decisions about timber harvest and other activities can be expected to affect populations of this secretive forest-dwelling raptor.

Queen Charlotte goshawks nest and hunt in large forests with big trees and an open canopy.

The olive-sided flycatcher is listed as a State of Alaska Species of Special Concern.

The four species of songbirds listed as Species of Special Concern are Neotropical migrants that winter in Central and South America. They migrate through Southeast in spring and fall, and some birds of each species nest here.

The **Townsend's warbler** is our most common breeding warbler, a striking bird with black and yellow markings that nests primarily in old growth forests. Not enough work has yet been done to establish long-term trends for Alaska, but we do know that populations of all four species have declined throughout their breeding ranges in the Lower 48 states. The declines are attributed mainly to loss of the birds' wintering habitat.

For example, in an account of the **olive-sided flycatcher**, John Wright of the Alaska Department of Fish and Game described the problem this way: "Mature evergreen forests of low- to mid-elevation in the Northern and Central Andes—[are] one of the most heavily altered habitats in South America. Andean valleys are almost completely deforested, and 85 percent or more of montane forests have been cut." This is an example of how the health of animal populations is often affected or determined by circumstances outside of Alaska.

The **harbor seal**, an animal many of us see from boats or from shore in Southeast, was listed as an Alaska Species of Special Concern because numbers of seals in some parts of Alaska have declined as much as 90 percent. The National Marine Mammal Laboratory and the Alaska Department of Fish and Game are now using aerial surveys, geographic information systems, and tagging with radio-frequency transmitters to study population trends, migration, and other aspects of harbor seal biology and behavior in different regions of Alaska.

In research at Glacier Bay funded by the National Park Service, Elizabeth Mathews, assistant professor of biology at the University of Alaska Southeast in Juneau, reported:

Since 1992 we have conducted aerial and shore-based surveys of harbor seals at glacial ice and terrestrial haulouts (resting areas). . . .Whereas seal numbers in southeastern Alaska had been considered stable, our data indicate that seal numbers in Glacier Bay declined by 35 to 50 percent between 1992 and 1999.

Legend for "Animals and Plants at Risk"

* Responsible agencies:

NMFS = National Marine Fisheries Service

ADF&G = Alaska Department of Fish and Game

USFWS = U.S. Fish and Wildlife Service

ANIMALS AND PLANTS AT RISK IN SOUTHEAST ALASKA

U. S. AND STATE OF ALASKA ENDANGERED SPECIES

Humpback Whale (NMFS*, ADF&G*)	The humpback whale is the species we usually see in Southeast. All other whale species migrate and feed along our outer coast, some far offshore. Commercial whaling decreased the number of these whales considerably, some almost to extinction. A ban on commercial whaling has resulted in numbers increasing but still, for many species, only a fraction of their pre-whaling population occurs today.
Northern right whale (NMFS, ADF&G)	
Sei whale (NMFS)	
Blue whale (NMFS, ADF&G)	
Fin whale (NMFS)	
Sperm whale (NMFS)	
Short-tailed albatross (USFWS*, ADF&G)	This albatross occurs mostly offshore in the Gulf of Alaska.
Leatherback sea turtle (NMFS)	This large sea turtle can weigh 6,000 lbs. About 17 have been sighted in SE.

U. S. THREATENED SPECIES

Steller sea lion (NMFS)	Rookeries at Forrester Is. (largest in world), White Sisters and Hazy Islands.
Steller's eider (USFWS)	This eider occasionally occurs in northern Southeast, especially Glacier Bay.
Snake River fall chinook salmon (NMFS)	Fish from these stocks of salmon from Washington, Idaho and Oregon may be taken incidentally in Southeast Alaska fisheries.
Lower Columbia River chinook salmon (NMFS)	
Upper Willamette River chinook salmon (NMFS)	
Green sea turtle (NMFS)	Only a few of these sea turtles have been sighted in Southeast Alaska waters.
Loggerhead sea turtle (NMFS)	
Olive (Pacific) ridley sea turtle (NMFS)	

STATE OF ALASKA SPECIES OF SPECIAL CONCERN

American peregrine falcon	Nests in the forested interior of Alaska, migrates through Southeast.
Arctic peregrine falcon	Nests in northern and western Alaska, migrates through Southeast.
Queen Charlotte goshawk	Nests and lives year-round in Southeast's old-growth forest.
Steller's eider	Also listed as a "Threatened" species under federal law.
Olive-sided flycatcher	These three bird species migrate through Southeast and some nest here.
Gray-cheeked thrush	
Blackpoll warbler	
Townsend's warbler	This bird is our most common breeding warbler in old-growth forests.
Steller sea lion	Also listed as a "Threatened" species under federal law.
Harbor seal	Inhabit entire Southeast coast, greatest numbers occur in Glacier Bay.
Chinook salmon (Fall Stock from Snake River)	Also listed as "Threatened" under federal law.

U.S. FOREST SERVICE SENSITIVE SPECIES

Trumpeter Swan	Nests in the Yakutat forelands and Chilkat River valley, winters Blind Slough.
Osprey	A rare bird here. Only 16 nests have been found in Southeast.
Queen Charlotte goshawk	Also listed as a State of Alaska "Species of Special Concern."
Peale's peregrine falcon	This subspecies nests in Southeast along the outer coast near seabird colonies.
Northern pike (Pike Lakes)	Only pike native to Southeast. Found in five lakes near Yakutat.
Chum salmon (Fish Creek)	Thought to be the largest chum salmon in North America (several over 38 lbs).
King salmon (Wheeler Creek)	These two king salmon runs from Admiralty Island are unique island genetic stocks. No other island runs are known to exist in Southeast.
King salmon (King Salmon River)	
Plants	
Eschscholtz's little nightmare (*Aphragmus eschscholtzianus*)	Found in subalpine and alpine habitat, perhaps in northern Southeast.
Norberg arnica (*Arnica lessingii ssp. norbergii*)	Found in meadows and open forest, known from the Yakutat area.
Goose-grass sedge (*Carex lenticularis var. dolia*)	Generally at high elevations, known from the Juneau and Ketchikan areas.
Edible thistle (*Cirsium edule*)	Open meadows, freshwater shores, found in Misty Fjords National Monument.
Pretty shooting star (*Dodecatheon pulchellum ssp. alaskanum*)	Occurs in wet meadows, found in northern Southeast.
Davy mannagrass (*Glyceria leptostachya*)	Found in shallow freshwater in Wrangell area.
Wright filmy fern (*Hymenophyllum wrightii*)	Found in coastal forest near Petersburg and Sitka.
Truncate quillwort (*Isoetes truncata*)	Occurs in shallow fresh water ponds, suspected throughout Southeast.
Calder lovage (*Ligusticum calderi*)	Found in alpine and subalpine habitat, occurs on Dall and Prince of Wales Is.
Pale poppy (*Papaver alboroseum*)	Grows in open habitat, suspected to occur in the Skagway and Juneau areas.
Bog orchid (*Platanthera gracilis*)	Grows on wet meadows and bogs, in the southernmost portion of Southeast.
Loose-flowered bluegrass (*Poa laxiflora*)	Grows on upper beach meadows and open forest from Hoonah south.
Kamchatka alkali grass (*Puccinellia kamtschatica*)	Grows on tidal flats and sea beaches in the northern half of Southeast.
Unalaska mist-maid (*Romanzoffia unalaschcensis*)	Grows in rocky outcrop areas, and along streambanks in Southeast.
Queen Charlotte butterweed (*Senecia moresbiensis*)	Occurs in southern half of SE. Grows in alpine and subalpine meadows.
Circumpolar starwort (*Stellaria ruscifolia ssp. aleutica*)	Grows along creeks in the mountains. Has been found in Yakutat area.

Mathews said her group hopes to address possible factors involved in the decline in seals, such as changes in prey availability.

U.S. Forest Service Sensitive Species

One other classification attempts to call attention to certain groups of animals and plants. U.S. Forest Service Sensitive Species are "those plants and animals whose population viability has been formally acknowledged by the Regional Forester as warranting concern within the Forest. These include species with populations and/or habitats that are reduced, restricted, or vulnerable to resource development, or, species requiring special management to maintain population viability."

Northern pike from the Pike Lakes near Yakutat are listed as a U.S. Forest Service Sensitive Species.

Among the U.S. Forest Service Sensitive Species are four stocks of fish that have special qualities or limited distribution in Southeast Alaska. The only **northern pike** native to Southeast Alaska are found in the five Pike Lakes about 23 miles east of Yakutat. These fish probably survived because the most recent glacial advance missed the Pike Lakes area. Very little is known about the life history or population numbers of these pike.

Chum salmon from Fish Creek near Hyder are thought to be the largest chum salmon in North America. Biologists have found several chums weighing more than 38 pounds there, and the average weight of chums from the creek is about 20 pounds, twice the average weight of chums elsewhere. In cooperation with the Alaska Department of Fish and Game, the Forest Service monitors this population closely and has a program to improve their habitat. This chum population has been stable or increasing, with escapements numbering more than 60,000 in some years.

The **king salmon of Wheeler Creek and King Salmon River on Admiralty Island** are unique island genetic stocks. Only one other naturally occurring stock of king salmon is known to exist on islands in Southeast Alaska. Although information on the status of these stocks is limited, recent escapement counts suggest the population is stable or slightly decreasing.

Sixteen species of plants have been designated Sensitive Species in the Tongass National Forest because they are rare or have very limited distribution. One rather spectacular looking species, **pale poppy** (*Papaver alboroseum*), is thought to occur in open areas in the vicinity of Skagway and Juneau. Another, the extremely inconspicuous, moss-like **Wright filmy fern** (*Hymenophyllum wrightii*) has been found in the dense coastal rainforest near Petersburg and Sitka.

Our knowledge of these plants is very limited, but state and federal agencies continue to study these and other species at risk as part of protecting the rich legacy of Southeast's natural world.●

Chilling Out

How Warm-Blooded Animals Survive Southeast Winters

On a cold night in February, on a mountainside in Southeast Alaska, the snow is six feet deep. The wind is blowing, and the temperature is about 10°F.

In a hollow beneath the roots of a huge old Sitka spruce, a female black bear lies with two newborn cubs. Pink and hairless, with their eyes still squeezed shut, the tiny newborns are snuggled against their mother's warm belly. She is curled around them, holding them against her with the furry warmth of her front and hind legs.

For the next several months the cubs will live in the shelter of the den, squirming over their mother's body and greedily drinking her rich, fatty milk.

The sow will barely waken. She will not eat, sleep, or relieve herself. Her body temperature has dropped four to five degrees (Fahrenheit) below normal, and her heart may beat only 10 or 12 times a minute. Unless disturbed, she will stay this way until early May. Then she will gradually awaken, and the cubs—with thick coats of fur and weighing about five pounds each—will follow her out of the den into the forest that will be their summer home.

Above the bears' den, where not even the scrawniest trees survive, snow covers the boulders at the foot of an old avalanche chute. Beneath them a female marmot and her young of the previous summer are curled within the shelter of her snug

Chickadees survive all winter long in Southeast Alaska partly because they can spend nighttime in a state of torpor. They can rest, chilled below their normal body temperatures, then recover to forage during daylight.

underground burrow. All are still, except when they occasionally turn to stretch or shift position.

The marmots' body temperatures have dropped drastically below normal, and their hearts are beating only four to five times a minute.

Down at the foot of the mountain, a 200-year-old forest stretches toward the icy shore. Inside the gray skeleton of an ancient hemlock tree seven chickadees huddle together in a small cavity. They have found a nest hole carved into the tree's rotten heartwood the previous summer by red-breasted sapsuckers.

The chickadees are resting at body temperatures about 18°F below normal. They will stay in the cavity all night until daylight wakes them to forage for the seeds, spiders, and insect larvae that will carry them through the chilling cold of one more winter day.

Hypothermia, or lowering of the body's core temperature, is a deadly threat to nearly all warm-blooded animals, including humans.

But the bear, the marmot, and the chickadees are surviving precisely because their bodies are in that condition. Chilled below their normal body temperatures, they have

slowed down or stopped their physical activity and virtually all their bodily functions.

Each animal, in its own way, is conserving energy and cutting back its food requirements as a way to survive the cold and food shortages of winter. How the animals manage to do this—through carefully regulated processes known as hibernation, deep sleep, and short-term torpor (nearly total mental and physical inactivity)—is one of the marvels of nature.

We are only beginning to understand how these processes work and what remarkable implications these animals' use of regulated hypothermia may have for human beings.

The True Hibernators

Two animals in Southeast Alaska are considered "true hibernators"—hoary marmots, found throughout mainland Southeast, and arctic ground squirrels, found in the coastal mountains north of Skagway.

Each winter these small mammals hole up in sheltered places for as long as six to eight months. Though they may wake occasionally, they primarily sleep. Their body temperatures decline drastically; heartbeat, blood pressure, and oxygen consumption decrease; and much of the time the animals appear to be comatose or even dead. Yet, when spring approaches, something changes. The animals wake up and resume their normal activities.

How do they do it?

Both marmots and ground squirrels eat voraciously in late summer and early fall, often doubling their normal weight. Much of the increase takes the form of fat, which provides twice as much energy as carbohydrate. This gives the animals enough built-in energy to function at a reduced level as they sleep away the winter.

Marmots and ground squirrels also take shelter from the weather in underground burrows—another way to save energy and

Hoary marmots spend the winter hibernating in underground burrows, emerging in the spring to feed on succulent vegetation.

protect themselves during the months they will be mostly inactive.

When marmots enter their burrows for the winter, they plug the entrance to their sleeping chamber with dirt, vegetation, and feces. This blocks out predators such as wolves and prevents the loss of heat, like closing and weatherstripping the door to your house in winter. Layers of earth and snow over the burrow provide insulation from wind and cold, so ambient temperatures in the burrows nearly always stay at least a few degrees above freezing, regardless of the temperatures outside.

Once inside their burrows, the true hibernators allow their bodies to drop into regulated hypothermia gradually, decreasing their activity over several days.

Arctic ground squirrels go into deeper hibernation than any other animal, and much research has been done on them, particularly in northern Alaska.

Researchers at the University of Alaska Fairbanks found the body temperatures of hibernating arctic ground squirrels could drop from a normal 98°F to as low as 34 or 35°F. This is remarkable since the hearts of non-hibernating mammals will not beat at all at temperatures below about 50 to 70°F.

The squirrels' heartbeats also slowed from a normal 350 beats a minute to an extraordinary two to four beats a minute. That would decrease blood flow to the brain by an estimated 80 or 90 percent—a decrease that in nonhibernating mammals would damage or destroy crucial nerve cells within minutes.

Scientists think hibernators get away with this because their metabolic rate also drops, sometimes as much as 98 to 99 percent, and cellular processes slow down significantly.

Blood flow to the extremities slows in hibernating animals as well, but certain parts of the nervous system continue to regulate the animals' metabolism as temperatures drop. That includes parts that perceive changes in the environment, so if the environment gets too cold, the animals will wake up or increase their metabolism to warm up (something that humans suffering from hypothermia cannot do).

Marmots are believed to wake occasionally during the winter, but they rouse slowly, perhaps taking as long as two hours to regain normal body temperature. Arctic ground squirrels wake for a day or so every three weeks or less. Waking seems to be essential so the animals can remove accumulated wastes that would otherwise poison their bodies.

Arctic ground squirrels are considered "true hibernators." During hibernation their body temperatures may drop to 34 degrees F. and their metabolic rate may drop as much as 99 percent.

The Bears' "Long Sleep"

Human beings in northern climates have long been aware that brown and black bears hibernate for the winter. Like marmots and arctic ground squirrels, bears lay on heavy layers of fat each late summer and fall. They spend the winter in dens, sheltered from wind, rain, and cold.

But the bears' "long sleep" is different from that of the true hibernators. The bears' body temperatures do not drop as drastically. Their metabolism does not slow as much. And unlike true hibernators, bears can wake from their "sleep" and become active almost immediately.

In 1998 Brian Barnes and Oivind Toien, biologists at the University of Alaska Fairbanks Institute of Arctic Biology, studied two black bears that hibernated on the university campus. The three-year-old female bear and a yearling male, captured as problem bears at Elmendorf Air Force Base near Anchorage, were put in a padded box where they were monitored for heartbeat, shivering, breathing, and brain wave patterns.

The scientists found the bears' body temperatures dropped below their normal level of 99°F but never below about 85°F. Other studies have found bears' metabolic rate drops to only about 50 percent of the normal level.

These changes are not as extreme as those undergone by true hibernators, but they are enough to save considerable energy through the winter. It is believed bears do not "sleep" as deeply because it would take too long for such large animals to cool down and warm up again.

Bears do not urinate or defecate for the whole time they are asleep in their dens. This has especially intrigued scientists who wonder how the animals can survive for six to eight months without excreting harmful bodily wastes.

Studies have found that urea is produced in the liver, released into the blood, and excreted in saliva, which the animals swallow. When urea reaches the intestine, bacteria convert it back into bicarbonate and ammonia. Other bacteria convert the ammonia into protein. The ammonia is completely recycled. The bears' bodily wastes are degraded and reabsorbed.

The Short-Term Torpor of Chickadees

Chickadees, one of a number of songbird species that overwinter in Alaska, use regulated hypothermia in yet a different way. Unlike marmots, ground squirrels, and bears, they cannot store up enough fat to carry them through weeks or months of hibernation. So instead they forage during the day, then save energy by allowing their body temperatures to drop during the night.

When roosting chickadees turn down their internal thermostats, their normal body temperature may drop from about 108°F to 90°F. Peter Marchand, author of the fascinating book *Life in the Cold,* explains that chickadees do this by controlling shivering.

Like most birds, chickadees shiver a lot in winter, using that muscle movement to warm themselves up. But, Marchand writes, chickadees do even more:

> *By controlling shivering through shorter and less frequent shivering outbreaks, body temperature gradually drops until a particular depth of hypothermia (varying seasonally) is reached. Shivering is then resumed with regular bursts, maintaining a closely regulated hypothermia.*

On a cold winter night the bird thus saves 20 percent of the energy normally required to maintain body temperature.

Chickadees do put on an amazing amount of extra fat in winter, according to Pierre Deviche and Susan Sharbaugh, two researchers at the University of Alaska Fairbanks.

The biologists found that in winter the birds seemed to eat as much as they could during the day. In fact, they gained the equivalent of 10 percent of their body weight in fat, then burned virtually all of it up during the night.

Imagine a person who weighed 150 pounds eating enough to gain 15 pounds in a day, then burning it off during the night and waking up weighing 150 again in the morning. "It's a huge physiological feat," Sharbaugh said.

Nest holes excavated by red-breasted sapsuckers in summer make perfect shelters for small resident birds such as chickadees and brown creepers in winter.

Like marmots and ground squirrels, chickadees seek out places where they can shelter and hide from predators during their torpor.

When he was on Admiralty Island studying forest habitat near Hawk Inlet, Alaska biologist Jeff Hughes watched chickadees and other small birds piling into cavities in large old trees and snags at the end of the day. Hughes wrote in an article for *Natural History* magazine:

> *Since nights may be sixteen hours long, and the birds typically roost from before sunset to sunrise, chickadees, creepers, and hairy woodpeckers essentially spend most of the winter in these tree holes. A single hole often contains more than one bird and may be crowded with roostmates of a few different species.*

Hughes found the temperature inside an occupied cavity can be six to 11°F higher than the temperature outdoors, even in weather below freezing. Combined with a daytime buildup of fat and nighttime regulated hypothermia, these shelters must help birds save tremendous amounts of energy during winter. ●

Anna's hummingbirds are rare in Southeast Alaska. They are more often seen at sugar water feeders in the fall.

Eagle's Torpor

An Anna's hummingbird showed up at my Juneau home one cold day in October. I lured him inside because the flowers were gone and the sugar water in the outside feeder was in danger of freezing. I kept him alive with a mixture of Similac, sugar, fish food flakes, and water.

I was to keep him for about a month, then someone from the Alaska Raptor Center in Sitka was going to take him to a hummingbird rehabilitation facility in San Diego. I named him Eagle.

Eagle seemed content having the run of my dining room. He would go into torpor at dusk and awaken at daybreak. Indoor lights did not alter this pattern.

During torpor he appeared oblivious to any activity around him. I could move about, rattle dishes, or talk, and he would remain perfectly still on his perch. He appeared stiff, with his neck pulled down, his eyes closed, and his bill pointing up in the air.

When it was time for Eagle to be carried south, I captured him in the middle of the night while he was still in torpor. His body seemed lifeless; he did not move or open his eyes. However, the whole time I held him he uttered a pitiful squeaking sound.

Hummingbirds have the highest metabolic rate and the greatest metabolic range of any vertebrate. The ability to go into torpor helps them to conserve energy and may be critical to their survival.

In general, they are capable of lowering their body temperature to that of the surrounding air during torpor. This is quite a feat since their daytime activity temperature is about 104° F.

As the birds wake from torpor, their temperature increases about 2° F per minute. This means that a torpid hummingbird in Southeast would require about 27 minutes to fully awaken from an overnight temperature of 50° F to its normal operating temperature of 104° F.

To Freeze
or
Not To Freeze

How Cold-Blooded Animals Survive Southeast Winters

Imagine it's mid-winter in Southeast Alaska. The temperature has been in the low 40s for several days, and it's been raining. The ground is bare. Then one day the skies clear and the temperature plummets—to 20 degrees, 10 degrees, or even zero.

Warm-blooded animals have developed a number of ways to cope with such cold. They can generate considerable body heat by themselves, and they are covered with fur or feathers that help them control heat loss. Bears and marmots may already be hibernating in sheltered dens. Chickadees may crowd together in old woodpecker holes and fall into torpor to get through the night. And sea ducks such as scoters and harlequins are insulated by thick layers of fat and down, and covered with outer coats of interlocking feathers that repel wind and water.

But what about cold-blooded animals that have no protective coats and whose body temperatures generally fluctuate with their surroundings? What about wood frogs that cannot dig into the ground—butterflies and other wintering insects barely protected in the cracks of tree bark—intertidal invertebrates such as barnacles and mussels exposed to freezing temperatures and wind chill for several hours between tides?

If you can't get away from the cold, the solution comes down to one tough choice: To freeze or not to freeze. Figure out a way your body can counteract freezing temperatures, or give in and figure out how to survive being frozen alive!

Many spiders are resistant to cold. You can often see them running about on the snow.

A number of cold-blooded animals in Southeast Alaska cope with this dilemma every winter—mourning cloak butterflies, snow mosquitoes (those big ones that emerge earliest in the spring), the insect larvae that live in willow "roses" (those roundish galls often found at the tips of willow branches), and spiders that crawl about on snow.

Why worry about freezing?

Freezing is lethal to living things for a number of reasons. Ice crystals in body tissues can deform cells and puncture cell and capillary walls, much as water that becomes frozen will bulge out and split a plastic container. Freezing sucks water out of cells into growing ice crystals, leaving the cells shrunken and damaged (think of freezer-burned meat or fish). Freezing also prevents blood from delivering oxygen and nutrients throughout the body, so the organs become damaged as, for example, a human suffers a stroke when a blood clot blocks oxygen from reaching the brain.

So in winter many cold-blooded animals take shelter to reduce the intensity of cold they may have to face—hiding under leaf litter, beneath roof shingles on our houses, or in unheated buildings. But freezing tem-

peratures could still penetrate their shelters, so they have developed a number of other survival mechanisms that involve complex chemical and biological changes in their bodies.

Ways to avoid freezing

Many spiders and insects—including snow mosquitoes and the willow gall larva—have developed ways to keep from freezing even at temperatures below those at which their body fluids would normally freeze. By building up extremely high concentrations of sugars or sugar alcohols in their blood and tissues, they lower the freezing point of their body fluids, much the way antifreeze lowers the freezing point of water in a car radiator.

The animals produce these substances from the large carbohydrate reserves they've accumulated during summer and fall feeding, and their production is prompted by declining temperatures and perhaps decreasing hours of daylight. In midwinter the level of glycerol in the arctic willow gall insect (*Rhabdophaga* spp.), for example, may account for as much as 20 percent of the larva's body weight.

Many insects also can produce another type of antifreeze—special proteins that bind to the surface of any ice crystals beginning to develop in the blood and keep them from growing. This not only keeps the crystals small and harmless. It also causes them to grow as smooth, hexagonal disks, so they have less potential for damaging cells than sharp, spiky crystals do.

Animals that seek to avoid freezing may use other strategies to add to the effectiveness of antifreeze substances. They might lose significant amounts of water, which raises the proportion of dissolved substances in their bodies and lowers their freezing point. They may also eliminate or reduce the number of particles in their bodies that ice crystals might use as nuclei around which to

(Far left) Larvae of the willow gall insect (a species of fly) winter inside round abnormal growths that emerge when the young larvae infest the tips of willow branches. These growths, or "roses," have an outer protective layer and an inner layer that the larvae feed upon.

(Inset) Willow gall larvae, like the one indicated with an arrow in the photo, keep from freezing by building up high concentrations of sugars or sugar alcohols in their blood and tissues.

grow. Since any small particle can serve as a nucleus for freezing to begin, some insects empty their guts in the fall, eliminating digestive microbes, food particles, and foreign mineral material or dust that could serve as nuclei. Others somehow "mask" the particles within cell organelles or membranes so they can't serve as nuclei.

For animals trying to avoid freezing, ice or water particles in the external environment can also serve as "flashpoints" for freezing. So these creatures select dry hibernation sites, or protect themselves with a waxy cuticle on the outside of their bodies, or spin waterproof cocoons, or live encased in galls that grow around them when they secrete potent chemicals on host plants.

A few other animals, however, have adopted an "if you can't fight 'em, join 'em" strategy. Their approach may be the most remarkable of all because these animals have to cope with being frozen alive.

Giving in and freezing alive

A number of insects, including certain beetles, flies, bees, and ants, manage to survive freezing because they confine the ice to spaces between, rather than within, the cells of their bodies. Like animals that *avoid* freezing, they build up high concentrations of sugars or sugar alcohols that serve as antifreeze *within* their cells, but ice forms in the fluid *outside* the cells, where it can't bulge the cells out or puncture their critical membranes. As the ice forms, it sucks water out of the cell interiors and leaves behind an increasingly thick and syrupy solution. The thickening solution further lowers the freezing point and provides support so that cell walls are less likely to collapse and be damaged.

In winter wood frogs can freeze for months, with no heartbeat, circulation, breathing, or muscle movement. Come spring, the frogs thaw and "come back to life."

"Freeze-tolerant" insects also *promote* freezing in the spaces outside their cells. They produce special "ice nucleators" that cause ice to begin forming in their bodies as soon as the temperature drops a few degrees below freezing. As a result, their bodies freeze slowly, taking up to 48 hours for maximum ice accumulation, and their metabolisms have time to adjust to their frigid state.

Wood frogs take a slightly different tack. While they confine freezing to areas outside their cells as the insects do, frogs freeze up at least twice as fast.

As soon as the first ice crystals begin to form on its skin, the wood frog's body produces massive amounts of glucose, a blood sugar, and dumps it into the bloodstream at an extraordinary rate—reaching perhaps 200 times the normal level within about eight hours. Within one minute after freezing begins, the frog's heartbeat may double, so glucose is rapidly carried to all the body tissues while extracellular freezing is progressing. Twenty hours or less after freezing

began, the frog's heart will have stopped and its breathing will have ceased.

Janet and Kenneth Storey, researchers at Carleton University in Ottawa, Canada, have done extensive studies of freezing in wood frogs. Here's how they describe what happens to frogs they've observed:

> *Ice penetrates through all of the fluid compartments of the animal and within just a few hours a mass of ice fills the abdominal cavity, encasing all the internal organs. Large, flat ice crystals run between the layers of skin and muscle, and the eyes turn white because the lens freezes. Their blood stops flowing and as much as 65% of the frog's total body water is converted to ice. Breathing, heart beat, and muscle movements all stop and the frozen 'frogsicle' exists in a virtual state of suspended animation until it thaws.*

Scientists are still studying how frogs' body functions are reactivated once thawing begins, but they have found that within an hour after thawing, the frog's heart resumes beating, and six hours later at a temperature of only 41°F the animal's heart rate may be back to normal. According to the Storeys:

> *Frozen frogs can survive for weeks with no heartbeat, no circulation, no breathing, and no muscle movement. Yet, within only a few minutes after thawing is complete, heartbeat resumes, then the frog begins to gulp for air, and then soon blinks, stretches and pushes itself up into a sitting position.*

Here's another remarkable thing about the frogs: the antifreeze substance they build up is glucose, the normal blood sugar of all vertebrates, rather than glycerol, the substance that most freeze-tolerant insects build up. Freezing wood frogs can easily tolerate blood sugar levels 100 or 200 times

for transplant. If we could learn to preserve donor organs for weeks or months rather than merely hours, many human lives could be saved. There are even implications for agriculture, for insects that naturally control crop pests could be produced in large numbers, then frozen and held in suspended animation until the proper season to release them.

So if you see a mourning cloak butterfly glide past on a warm March day, or as you prepare to swat a big spring snow mosquito that's landed on your arm, stop for a minute. It might be interesting to think about the amazing mechanisms these animals used to get through the winter.●

Illustration by Katherine Hocker

normal, but they show none of the problems human diabetics suffer when their blood sugar increases only twice or 10 times above normal.

How do they do it? If we can find out, that information could be useful in treating human diabetes.

There are other implications. Research on how animals regulate and recover from freezing is especially interesting to scientists studying the logistics of preserving organs

Mourning cloak butterfly

Life
in the High
Country

The country above tree line in Southeast Alaska is a mosaic of stunning variety. Most Southeast peaks are steep and craggy. Barren ridges stretch between them, buffeted by wind and wrapped in snow fields, sunlight, or clouds of fog, even in summer. But in small valleys and on gentler slopes, fields of wildflowers billow across the ground during summer. Hardy plants cluster in sheltered hollows or spring up wherever their roots can take hold. At times the slopes are virtually rock gardens bursting with color.

A remarkable variety of animals live in this terrain or pass through it enroute to other areas. Birds and insects reap its seasonal treasures. And mammals such as marmots, bears, and deer graze on the lush vegetation in subalpine meadows.

Here, up close, are some residents of high country we especially enjoy:

(Above) Blue grouse overlooking Juneau

(Left) Rock ptarmigan are the most commonly seen ptarmigan in high country. Females change from white to brown plumage early in summer, but males (like this one) take longer, perhaps to be more visible for courtship or to help lure predators away.

Hoary marmots love rocky places, especially outcrops near lush meadows. There they sun themselves and waddle about like overfed squirrels, eating the grasses, flowers, sedges, berries, and roots nearby. They excavate burrows or find natural crannies for nesting and protection from predators. At times marmots seem to be very playful. They may chase each other, tumble around on the ground, and even box, standing erect on their hind paws and pushing each other with their palms.

Mountain goats often winter at or below tree line. In summer they move up to high mountain meadows, where they graze on herbs, grasses, and low-growing shrubs.

Some of the most abundant high country plants are heathers. At high elevations moisture is tied up in snow most of the year, and at other times the unforgiving wind pulls it quickly from plants and the soil. But these heathers have thick, waxy leaves with undercurled edges that hold moisture within the plant.

White mountain-heather and yellow mountain-heather grow low to the ground out of the wind, often forming extensive mats over the thin, nutrient-poor soil.

The two to three months that summer lasts in high country is not much time for plants to flower and produce seeds. Some plants save time and energy by sending out runners underground and starting new plants from them.

Alpine bistort produces tiny bulblets below its flowers. The bulblets fall from the plant, ready to sprout into new plants complete with an initial supply of stored food.

Some alpine plants, like this **moss campion**, grow in closely packed cushion shapes low to the ground. This allows them to conserve precious moisture and warmth. One study showed that air can be up to 40 degrees warmer within the cushion than it is several inches above the plant.

One of the latest blooming high country flowers is the **broad-petalled gentian**. You can see its blossoms clear into fall when other flowers have died back. Sometimes it grows in large patches, especially in wet or moist areas. Its blossoms close on cloudy days and open on sunny days.

Though alpine plants are often smaller than their counterparts at lower elevations, they may still produce relatively large blossoms. Scattered as they often are in crevices, nooks, and crannies, they must shout to potential pollinators, "Hey — look what I've got over here!" These brilliant pink flowers are **wedge-leafed primrose**, sometimes called "pixie eyes."

Alpine monkshood is found in a wide range of habitats, from open forests and stream banks to alpine ridges and meadows.

Alpine monkshood plants are generally small and produce single flowers, while monkshood that grow in the valley tend to grow considerably taller, with 10 or more flowers to a plant.

Common ravens are at home in all habitats, from sea level to high country, but high country is a good place to watch their playfulness and tremendous flight capabilities.

Mountain harebell is another plant that grows smaller and has a single blossom in the alpine. Like the wedge-leafed primrose, its blossom is large in relation to the rest of the plant, which helps attract pollinators.

Luetkea, or "partridgefoot," is very common in the alpine, often spreading to form a kind of evergreen mat over the ground. Its leaves crowd together at the base, and after withering may persist for many years. The plant is also known as "creeping spirea" or "mountain spirea."

White-tailed ptarmigan live mostly at higher elevations than rock and willow ptarmigan do.

Golden-crowned sparrows (right) often nest among taller willows and alders just above timberline.

One of the most common birds seen in Southeast high country is the **American pipit** (above). Pipits feed mostly on insects. Like other alpine birds they give their soft, tinkling song in flight, in essence announcing "I'm here!" in the way that birds of the forest do from perches on treetops or lower branches.

Pipits commonly nest on the ground above tree line on drier ridges.

The **gray-crowned rosy finch** (above) is a distinctive bird with a canary-like warble. Rosy finches nest in cliff crevices and rock slides and give a harsh *cheep-cheep* sound in flight. They are often found on snow patches, where they feed on insects grown sluggish from the cold.

Golden eagles are basically alpine hunters. They sweep across mountain ridges and slopes, flying near ground level to capture marmots and ptarmigan to feed themselves and their young.

They usually nest on cliff ledges.

Sex on the Mountain

Illustration by Jim Fowler

Have you ever hiked up to a mountaintop in Southeast on a sunny, warm summer day, and found yourself surrounded by buzzing insects? That happened to me one day when I hiked to the top of Mt. Troy on Douglas Island with a number of friends.

We had climbed up from the Eaglecrest Ski Area and had surely earned a good rest, but as we settled down on the rocks to eat our lunch and enjoy the view, dozens of insects of all shapes and sizes were zooming about. Many of them seemed to be chasing each other, and occasionally they would land on us (Maybe they were out of breath!).

My friends spent a lot of energy swatting and slapping, worried that they were going to be eaten alive.

Fortunately, I had just read a book called *Mountains and Northern Forests* by two Canadian naturalists, Richard and Sydney Cannings, and I knew the insects were not very likely to bite us at all. They were up on the mountain for other reasons.

According to the Cannings, it's pretty difficult for some male and female insects to find each other in the forest, so some of them—particularly strong flyers like certain flies, butterflies, and moths—intuitively head uphill, where their chances of a rendezvous are better than down in the forest.

The Cannings wrote:

Generally speaking, males fly to hilltops and stay there, waiting for females. The females fly up for brief visits only—they quickly find a mate and then journey back down to their particular habitat on the hillside or in the valley, where they lay their eggs.

The Cannings also pointed out that high places like mountaintops are also just about the only place you will ever see male horse flies—gorgeously handsome creatures that have one big advantage over their female counterparts—They don't bite!

Knowing the creatures buzzing around me were only interested in sex, I was able to relax and calmly admire them as they landed and crawled about on my bare arms and legs. They were fascinating! Some had long, dangly legs. Some had yellow bands around their abdomens like some kind of wasp.

Some of the big ones (probably male horseflies) had beautiful, translucent wings and big fluorescent eyes on the top of their heads.

I tried to convince my fellow hikers that the insects meant them no harm. "They're just interested in sex, not you," I said. But it was to no avail. They kept waving the insects away, probably unable to believe the critters were more interested in each other than in a good meal.●

Index

Acknowledgments

Like all Southeast Alaskans, we are deeply indebted to the researchers who have contributed so much to our knowledge of the natural world we enjoy. All those we contacted were unfailingly generous in sharing their time to answer questions and explain their work. Some, such as Mary Willson, shared information on a wide variety of topics and inspired us to explore new directions. Among them, we would especially like to thank: Koren Bosworth, Edmund D. "Butch" Brody, Jr., Edmund D. Brody III, Bill and Lorene Calder, Richard Carstensen, Scott Gende, Tom Hanley, Al Harris, Jack Helle, Robert Hodge, John Hudson, Jeff Hughes, Mike Jacobsen, Jim King, Gary Laursen, Steve Lewis, Kim Obermeyer, John Schoen, Mark Schultz, Greg Streveler, and Dustin Wittwer.

For four and a half years, as we wrote and researched most of the stories that evolved into this book, the staff of the *Alaskan Southeaster* encouraged us and helped us look good in print. We are grateful to: Dave Fremming, Bill DeArmond, Mary Lou Gerbi, Jenny Whittemore, Beth McLean, Elizabeth Knecht, and Cindy Ruby.

For companionship on the trail and other support and encouragement, thanks to Rich Gordon, Mike Larsen, Beth & Ken Melville, Tom Osborn, Cynthia Puig, Barb Short, Pauline Strong, Flip Todd; Debbie Reifenstein, Susan Hickey, and Katrina Pearson at Hearthside Books; and all the neighbors who share with us their stories and questions about the natural world.